STUDIES IN OLD TESTAMENT SACRIFICE

STUDIES IN OLD TESTAMENT SACRIFICE

ROLAND DE VAUX, O.P.

CARDIFF
UNIVERSITY OF WALES PRESS
1964

PRINTED IN GREAT BRITAIN
AT THE UNIVERSITY PRESS, OXFORD
BY VIVIAN RIDLER
PRINTER TO THE UNIVERSITY

To

AUBREY R. JOHNSON

in token of esteem

and friendship

PREFACE

THIS volume contains in a somewhat expanded form the four Elizabeth James Lectures which I had the honour to give at University College, Cardiff, in October 1961. They were not intended to be—and this book is not—a complete and systematic study of Old Testament sacrifice and its place in the cult. They were studies of the origin, history, and religious significance of the different sacrifices prescribed by the Old Testament laws or practised by the Israelites.

In this historical perspective, two aspects are thrown in relief: as might be expected, most of the rites of the Old Testament sacrifices were inherited from the earlier nomadic phase (Passover, blood rites) or borrowed from neighbours (holocaust, communion sacrifice). But—and this is the second point—the historical and moral character of the religion of Israel modifies these foreign forms of cult and gives them a new value: Passover becomes a memorial of the salvation of the people, holocaust and communion sacrifice lose the meaning that they bore among the Canaanites of meals offered to the god, and expiatory sacrifices respond to a new religious imperative, the need for pardon from God for transgression of the divine law. Conversely, sacrificial forms which were contrary to the true spirit of religion (sacrifices to Moloch), though indulged in by the Israelites, were strongly condemned by the authorized representatives of Yahwism.

The unique sacrifice of Christ has rendered obsolete the sacrificial rites of the Old Testament but these had played their part as an expression of the piety of our ancestors in faith and as a means of their sanctification. Moreover, the teaching of the Old Testament has not lost its value for Christians. By partaking in Christ's sacrifice they fulfil the fundamental obligation of worship, thanksgiving, and expiation which the Old Testament sacrifices were already intended to satisfy.

It is a pleasant duty to thank the Senate and Council of University College, Cardiff, for the honour they have conferred on me in inviting me, and for their hospitality to me on this occasion. I am specially indebted to the Reverend Professor Aubrey R. Johnson, who so kindly sponsored me and made my stay in Cardiff so pleasant. Last but not least, I wish to thank my friends who helped in preparing these lectures for publication: Fathers Joseph Bourke and Roland Potter, who undertook to translate the lectures from my French manuscript, and Mrs. Crystal M. Bennett and Mr. Donald Boalch, who checked the translation.

R. DE VAUX, O.P.

Oxford, Blackfriars
October 1962

CONTENTS

PRINCIPAL ABBREVIATIONS

A.f.O.	*Archiv für Orientforschung*
A.J.S.L.	*American Journal of Semitic Languages and Literatures*
B.Z.	*Biblische Zeitschrift*
C.B.Q.	*Catholic Biblical Quarterly*
C.I.S.	*Corpus Inscriptionum Semiticarum*
C.R.A.I.	*Comptes-rendus de l'Académie des Inscriptions et Belles-Lettres*
C.T.	*Cuneiform Texts* (London)
F.H.G.	*Fragmenta Historicorum Graecorum*
H.U.C.A.	*Hebrew Union College Annual*
J.A.	*Journal Asiatique*
J.B.L.	*Journal of Biblical Literature*
J.P.O.S.	*Journal of the Palestine Oriental Society*
J.S.S.	*Journal of Semitic Studies*
J.T.S.	*Journal of Theological Studies*
M.U.B.	*Mélanges de l'Université de Beyrouth*
P.E.Q.	*Palestine Exploration Quarterly*
R.A.	*Revue d'Assyriologie et d'Archéologie Orientale*
R.B.	*Revue Biblique*
R.E.J.	*Revue des Études Juives*
R.G.G.	*Die Religion in Geschichte und Gegenwart*
R.H.R.	*Revue de l'Histoire des Religions*
T.C.L.	*Textes Cunéiformes du Louvre*
T.L.Z.	*Theologische Literaturzeitung*
V.T.	*Vetus Testamentum*
W.Z.K.M.	*Wiener Zeitschrift für die Kunde des Morgenlandes*
Z.A.	*Zeitschrift für Assyriologie*
Z.A.W.	*Zeitschrift für die alttestamentliche Wissenschaft*
Z.D.M.G.	*Zeitschrift der deutschen morgenländischen Gesellschaft*
Z.D.P.V.	*Zeitschrift des deutschen Palästina-Vereins*
Z.N.W.	*Zeitschrift für die neutestamentliche Wissenschaft*

I

THE PASSOVER SACRIFICE

DURING the New Testament period Passover was, as it has continued to be, the greatest of the Jewish festivals. But it was not always so. It is not mentioned among the three annual festivals of the ancient religious calendars found in Exodus xxiii and xxxiv, where we find only the feast of Unleavened Bread. It appears only in the additions to these calendars (Exod. xxiii. 18 and xxxiv. 25), and as separate from the three pilgrimage festivals. These additions, in which the feast is called a *ḥag*, a pilgrimage, are later than Deuteronomy, which first imposed the obligation of coming to the central sanctuary for Passover (Deut. xvi. 5–6). The first Passover so celebrated was the one which came as the culmination to Josiah's reform (2 Kings xxiii. 21–23), and the passage underlines the novelty of this practice: 'Such a Passover had not been celebrated since the time of the Judges . . . .'[1] Passover was not yet joined to the feast of Unleavened Bread, of which there is no mention in the account of Josiah's reform; the reference to the feast of Unleavened Bread in Deuteronomy xvi is secondary.[2] The connexion between Passover and the feast of Unleavened Bread does not appear before Leviticus xxiii. 5–8[3] and Ezekiel xlv. 21–24.

[1] The parallel passage in 2 Chron. xxxv. 18 says: 'since the time of Samuel'. This comes to the same thing, Samuel being considered as the last of the Judges in this tradition.

[2] The feast of Unleavened Bread is referred to in verses 3, 4*a*, and 8, but, if the people are to disperse on the morning following Passover night, verse 7, they cannot remain to eat the unleavened bread until the reunion on the seventh day, verse 8. On this history of Passover and the feast of Unleavened Bread cf. R. de Vaux, *Ancient Israel: Its Life and Institutions* (1961), pp. 484–93.

[3] In the Holiness Code, the basis of which goes back to the last years before the Exile. Cf. R. de Vaux, op. cit., pp. 143–4, 425–6, and 472–3.

1. *The Nomadic Character of the Earlier Passover*

However, in spite of these later developments, in spite of its omission from the first religious calendars, and the almost total silence of the historical books,[4] Passover is certainly very ancient. According to Joshua v. 10–12, it was celebrated at Gilgal at the first encampment in the Promised Land. Notwithstanding certain objections, which have recently been renewed,[5] an ancient tradition of the Gilgal sanctuary seems to be preserved in this passage, underlying a later redaction.[6] If this is correct, then the comment in 2 Kings xxiii. 22 and 2 Chronicles xxxv. 18 is substantiated, namely that Passover had not been celebrated communally in the one official sanctuary since the time of the Judges. At the period of the tribal confederation Passover was celebrated at the central sanctuary, the shrine of the ark.[7] The process of settlement led to a progressive loosening of tribal ties and to a dispersion of the cult, and during the period of the monarchy Passover became a family feast. This explains the silence of the calendars and the historical books.

Whatever judgements may be passed on Joshua v. 10–12,

[4] The only incontestable mention is the Passover of Josiah, 2 Kings xxiii. 21–23. The Passover of Hezekiah, described at length in 2 Chron. xxx, has no parallel in Kings; it is contradicted by 2 Kings xxiii. 22–23 and by the Chronicler himself, 2 Chron. xxxv. 18. The account presupposes that the fusion between Passover and the feast of Unleavened Bread had already been effected. This account appears to be a reconstruction by the Chronicler, who wished to give Hezekiah's religious reform (which is historical) the same solemn conclusion as that of Josiah's reform. Cf. M. Noth, *Überlieferungsgeschichtliche Studien I* (1943), p. 201; W. Rudolph, *Chronikbücher* (1955), *in loco*; H. Cazelles, *Les Livres des Chroniques*[2] (1961), *in loco*. The historicity of the account in Chron. is defended by S. Talmon, 'Divergences in Calendar Reckoning in Ephraim and Juda', in *V.T.* viii (1958), pp. 48–74, cf. pp. 58–63; H. J. Kraus, in *Evangelische Theologie* xviii (1958), pp. 63–65; H. Haag, art. 'Pâque', in *Supplément au dictionnaire de la Bible* vi (1960), col. 1133.

[5] E. Kutsch, 'Erwägungen zur Geschichte der Passafeier und des Massotfestes', in *Zeitschrift für Theologie und Kirche* lv (1958), pp. 1–35, cf. pp. 20–21.

[6] M. Noth, *Das Buch Josua*[2] (1953), pp. 11–12; H. W. Hertzberg, *Die Bücher Josua, Richter, Ruth* (1953), pp. 33–35; above all H. J. Kraus, 'Zur Geschichte des Passah-Massot-Festes im Alten Testament', in *Evangelische Theologie* xviii (1958), pp. 50, 54 ff., 59 ff.

[7] R. de Vaux, *Ancient Israel: Its Life and Institutions*, pp. 332 ff.

the actual rites of Passover bear witness to its antiquity. The most highly developed ritual is described in Exodus xii. This chapter is composite. It combines the Yahwist and priestly traditions, and its redaction has been influenced by the later history of Passover, and by its association with the Exodus from Egypt. The ritual which it describes, however, is clearly ancient. Passover is not described as a festival. It is a religious 'act'; one 'performs', *ʿāśāh*, the Passover (verse 48). It is a sacrifice, the sacrifice of Passover, *zeḇaḥ-pesaḥ* (verse 27). The Passover is immolated, *šāḥaṯ pesaḥ* (verse 21), the same word designating both rite and victim sacrificed. But this sacrifice is not performed in a sanctuary; it requires neither the presence of an altar nor the intervention of a priest. These aspects give Passover a place quite apart in Israelite ritual.

Originally Passover was a sacrifice of nomads or semi-nomads. That it has this character is generally recognized. However, some authors maintain that Passover is a practice of sedentary peoples. A. Vincent, who admits that Passover and the feast of Unleavened Bread were combined as early as the period of the Exodus, makes Passover a spring festival of agriculture.[8] S. H. Hooke considers it a New Year festival, and compares it with the Babylonian *akitu*.[9] This theory has been developed by I. Engnell.[10] According to this author, Passover is a spring festival of a type common among the ancient peoples of the Near East. It is a feast of sedentary peoples (the rite of smearing blood on the lintels and jambs of the doors of houses appears to him convincing evidence of this). It is a *ḥag*, a procession, in which the essential element consisted in a cultic 'exodus' to the desert, i.e. to the countryside, a 'cultic drama',[11] in which the chief part

[8] A. Vincent, *La Religion des Judéo-Araméens d'Éléphantine* (1937), pp. 306–7. He invokes the testimony of Philo, *Vita Mos. II* (III), 29, but Philo confuses Passover and the feast of Unleavened Bread, and no reliance can be placed on his late interpretation.

[9] S. H. Hooke, *The Origins of Early Semitic Ritual* (1938), pp. 48–50.

[10] I. Engnell, '*Paesaḥ-Maṣṣôt* and the Problem of "Patternism"', in *Orientalia Suecana* i (1952), pp. 39–50.

[11] In all essentials Engnell takes over J. Pedersen's interpretation of Exod. i–xv, cf. 'Passahfest und Passahlegende', in *Z.A.W.* lii (1934), pp. 161–75;

was played by the king, represented in the account of the Exodus by Moses. This would be a South Canaanite form of the New Year festival.

These opinions do not take sufficient account of the historical development of Passover and of its association with the feast of Unleavened Bread. Moreover they neglect the clear indications provided by the rites,[12] which are essentially: in each family an animal from the flocks, either a sheep or a goat, is slaughtered; the victim must be a male without blemish and one year old; the two jambs and the lintel of the house door are smeared with its blood; the victim is roasted whole over a fire with its head, feet, and entrails; it is eaten with unleavened bread and bitter herbs; none of the victim's bones must be broken, and nothing must be left; whatever has not been eaten by dawn must be burnt; those who eat it have their loins girt, sandals on their feet, and a staff in the hand. All these rites correspond to the customs of nomadic life, and certain of them can best be explained, or can *only* be explained, by these customs.

1. *The victim* (Exod. xii. 3, 5, 21)

This is a male from the flock. It is true that sheep and goats are also reared by sedentary peoples, and that they remained to the end the victims most often offered in Israelite sacrifices. But they are particularly suitable for semi-nomadic shepherds such as the forefathers of the Israelites were. The age of the victim is indicated by the phrase *ben-šānāh*, the exact sense of which is disputed. Taken literally the two terms can be understood to mean 'born within the year'.[13] In that case the phrase would refer to the period which had elapsed since the previous Passover,

id., *Israel: Its Life and Culture III–IV* (1940), 2nd ed. (1959), pp. 728–37. Cf. S. Mowinckel's criticism, 'Die vermeintliche "Passahlegende", Ex. 1–15, in Bezug auf die Frage: Literarkritik und Traditionskritik', in *Studia Theologica* v (1952), pp. 66–88, and Pedersen's reply in *Israel* . . . 2nd ed., pp. 794–5.

[12] Cf. E. Dhorme's brief and clear exposition, *L'Évolution religieuse d'Israël*, 'I. La Religion des Hébreux nomades' (1937), pp. 211–12.

[13] So Dhorme, op. cit., p. 211, and his translation in *La Bible de la Pléiade I* (1956).

and not to the calendar year. For since Passover was celebrated at the full moon of the first month (Exod. xii. 2), an animal fifteen days old at the most would not be suitable for a family meal to which it was expected that guests might be invited (Exod. xii. 4). Hebrew usage and parallel instances of this expression suggest that *ben-šānāh* should be understood as 'one year old'.[14] Finally it has been maintained that the term fixed the minimum age of the victim,[15] an interpretation which is philologically more difficult to defend. In any case the ordinary formula 'paschal lamb' is too narrow. All that is obligatory is that the victim shall be taken from the sheep or goats. It is possible that sheep were more often sacrificed, but goats would satisfy the prescriptions of the law equally well, and were never excluded by custom even in the New Testament period. It is even less certain that only young lambs were sacrificed.[16] 'Paschal lamb' is a Christian expression influenced by John i. 29, 'Behold the Lamb of God'. And this actually refers not to the Passover sacrifice, but to the Servant of Yahweh (Isa. liii. 7).[17]

Deuteronomy xvi. 2 extends the choice of Passover victim so as to include cattle too, and it is possible that this innovation was followed at Josiah's Passover (2 Kings xxiii. 21). The victims sacrificed on this occasion are recorded in 2 Chronicles xxxv. 7–9 and they include an impressive number of bullocks.[18] It is difficult to decide here whether the Chronicler has provided an exact record, or whether he is attesting a Second Temple practice on this point, or whether he is making use of the prescription in Deuteronomy to comment upon the laconic account of Kings. This last hypothesis is the most probable: indeed, the innovation of Deuteronomy has not been retained in the final redaction of the priestly law (Exod. xii. 3 and 5) nor does it appear in the practice of the New Testament period.

[14] So the majority of commentators and versions.

[15] G. B. Gray, *Sacrifice in the Old Testament: Its Theory and Practice* (1925), pp. 348 ff.

[16] Cf. Gray, op. cit., pp. 344 ff.

[17] Cf. what we say at the end of this chapter, p. 25.

[18] The same in 2 Chron. xxx. 24 for Hezekiah's Passover, on which cf. p. 2, n. 4.

Contrary to a fairly widespread view, there is nothing to show that Passover was an offering of the first-born of the flock.[19] Exodus xxxiv. 19 should not be adduced, for here the law of the first-born is inserted after the prescription for the feast of Unleavened Bread (Exod. xxxiv. 18), and not after the mention of the Passover victim, which is separated from it (Exod. xxxiv. 25*b*).[20] Moreover the law of the first-born is incompatible with the Passover ritual. For Passover has a fixed date, while the first-born should be offered on the eighth day after their birth (Exod. xxii. 28–29 (EVV. 29–30)). Again Exodus xii. 5, which lays down the exact qualities which the victim should have, would not have omitted to mention that it must be a first-born animal, had this characteristic been essential to the sacrifice.[21] It is true that the Passover of Exodus is linked to the tenth plague, which strikes all the first-born of Egypt (Exod. xii. 12–13, cf. verses 23, 27), and that the law of the first-born is joined to prescriptions on Passover (Exod. xiii. 1–2, 11–16). But this is a secondary association, derived from the manner in which Passover is inserted into the history of Salvation. Moreover, this association is an association by contrast: the first-born of the Israelites are spared by the plague.

2. *The ritual of blood* (Exod. xii. 7, 22)

In New Testament times the victim was first immolated by the offerer, and then the priests took its blood and poured it out at the foot of the altar. This custom was already being followed

[19] The opinion has recently been upheld by J. Henninger alike for the Israelite Passover and for the Arabic feasts of Rajab, of which we shall speak, 'Les Fêtes de printemps chez les Arabes et leurs implications historiques', in *Revista do Museu Paulista* (São Paulo) iv (1950), pp. 389–432; but he gives only arguments *de convenance*, and cannot cite any probative text. M.-J. Lagrange, *Études sur les religions sémitiques*[2] (1905), pp. 298–9, was more cautious: 'As this is the season when domestic animals normally bear their young, the first-born are included, without being the specific object of sacrifice.'

[20] Cf. N. M. Nicolsky, 'Pascha im Kulte des jerusalemischen Tempels', in *Z.A.W.* xlv (1927), pp. 174 ff.

[21] Cf. E. Kutsch, 'Erwägungen zur Geschichte der Passafeier und des Massotfestes', in *Zeitschrift für Theologie und Kirche* lv (1958), pp. 4–10, and 34.

at the time of the Chronicler according to 2 Chronicles xxx. 16, xxxv. 11. This rite can hardly be earlier than Deuteronomy. For when this code imposed the obligation of celebrating Passover at the Temple, it assigned to the altar and the priests a role which they did not originally play. This practice was a substitute for the rite prescribed both by Exodus xii. 22 (J) and by Exodus xii. 7 (P), a rite which the rabbis considered to be a particular prescription for the Passover of the Exodus, but which certainly constituted a constant element in the original Passover.

The blood of the victim was smeared on the lintel and the two jambs of the doors of houses where the Passover was eaten. I. Engnell[22] considers this mention of houses (cf. also verses 4, 13) a proof that Passover was a feast of sedentary peoples. One may reply[23] that semi-nomads, such as the ancestors of the Israelites were even in the patriarchal period, could have both fixed dwellings and tents at the same time.[24] Moreover the mention of houses is made necessary by the nature of the narrative, which describes this Passover in the context of the sojourn in Egypt. Finally, the ritual must have undergone some essential adaptation after the process of settlement in Canaan. An exact parallel is provided by the case of the Bedouin recently settled in the Kerak region. They offer sacrifices for the building of their houses and upon taking up residence in them. On such occasions the walls and lintels are anointed with blood.[25] But this is an adaptation of a Bedouin custom by which an animal is sacrificed whenever a new tent is put up, or when it is enlarged, or when its *ruag* (the fabric of the tent) is changed. The blood is then applied to the tent-poles and to the tent fabric.[26] Father Jaussen records the statement of a sheikh of Madaba: 'Each spring when I go out once more to take up my quarters in a tent, on the first

[22] In *Orientalia Suecana* i (1952), p. 46.

[23] H. Haag, 'Ursprung und Sinn der alttestamentlichen Paschafeier', in *Das Opfer der Kirche* (*Luzerner theologische Studien I*) (1954), p. 35.

[24] Gen. xxxiii. 17.

[25] A. Jaussen, *Coutumes des Arabes au pays de Moab* (1908), pp. 342–3. Similar rites are described by G. Dalman, *Arbeit und Sitte in Palästina VII* (1942), pp. 90 ff.

[26] A. Jaussen, op. cit., pp. 339–41.

evening I make a sacrifice (of several sheep), and straight away I sprinkle the posts and the *ruag* with blood.'[27]

Among the Arabs this rite has an apotropaic force. It is intended to preserve from all mischance those who set up a house or tent and are about to take up their abode in it. In certain cases the smearing with blood is extended to the animals of the flock.[28] In Exodus xii this apotropaic significance is most marked. The blood is a distinguishing sign on the houses of the Israelites and preserves them from the Destroyer, who wreaks havoc on that night. This is simply an application to the historical background of the Egyptian Passover of a motif which is fundamentally the same as in the Arabic parallels to which I have referred; I shall return to this point.

3. *The victim is roasted* (Exod. xii. 8, 9)

It is roasted by fire entire and whole. The Mishnah prescribes that it shall be roasted on a spit;[29] the Samaritans roast it in a pit dug in the earth. This practice is unique in the ritual of Israelite sacrifice, in which the victim was always cooked in a pot.[30] The sons of Eli were condemned for demanding that their portion of the sacrifices should be given to them in the form of meat for roasting instead of being taken from the pot where the victim's flesh was cooked (1 Sam. ii. 14–15). The text of Exodus xii. 9 underlines the exceptional character of this mode of preparing the Passover victim. This feature certainly derives from nomadism. Nomad shepherds do not encumber themselves with cooking utensils, and need only a fire to roast their meat. Here again Deuteronomy seeks to bring the Passover sacrifice into line with the rest of the ritual; it prescribes that the Passover victim must be cooked, just as in the communion sacrifices (Deut. xvi. 7). However, this reform did not prevail, as is proved by the directive in the Mishnah to which I have already referred.

[27] Ibid., p. 341.

[28] References in J. Henninger, loc. cit., p. 417. On the anointing of the animals of the flock cf. G. B. Gray, *Sacrifice . . .*, p. 300, quoting Doughty and Curtiss.

[29] Pes. vii. 1 ff.

[30] Cf. the laws of Exod. xxix. 31; Lev. viii. 31; Num. vi. 19; Ezek. xlvi. 24, and the account in Judges vi. 19.

4. *The bones are not broken* (Exod. xii. 46; cf. Num. ix. 12)

Parallels for this prescription are adduced from modern Arab custom. The Arabs themselves give various reasons for such practices. In the *'aqiqa* sacrifice, offered on the seventh day after the birth of a child, the bones of the victim are not broken in order to preserve the bones of the child from all accidents.[31] In the *edhedhiyeh* sacrifice in Palestine, and also in the sacrifice for the dead among the 'Oetabeh tribe, the bones of the victim are not broken because it is believed that the animal will serve as a mount on which the offerer may ride up to Paradise.[32]

Historians of religion suggest various explanations. The most widely accepted is that it was wished to ensure in this way that the bones of those taking part in the meal and the bones of the animals in their flocks would not be broken. Extending this inquiry to the nomad shepherds and hunters of central and northern Asia, where this custom is very widespread, J. Henninger[33] concludes that it stems from the idea that the bones are considered to be the support of the soul. By preserving them intact, the re-birth or survival of the animal or of the flock, and also of the participants at the sacrifice, is assured. He finds the same concept among modern Arabs, who regard the sacrificed animal as a prepared means of ascent to Paradise. He finds the same concept in the Bible, in those passages which designate the bones as an essential part of man, and the seat of his principle of life, cf. the very similar text of Psalms xxxiv. 21 (EVV. 20), also Psalms xxxi. 11 (EVV. 10); xxxii. 3; li. 10 (EVV. 8); Lamentations iii. 4, and the vision of dry bones revivified in Ezekiel xxxvii.[34] In

[31] S. I. Curtiss, *Ursemitische Religion im Volksleben des heutigen Orients* (1903), p. 201.

[32] T. Canaan, *J.P.O.S.* vi (1926), p. 41; J. Hess, *Z.A.W.* xxxv (1915), p. 130.

[33] J. Henninger, 'Zum Verbot des Knochenzerbrechens bei den Semiten', in *Studi Orientalistici in onore di Giorgio Levi della Vida I* (1956), pp. 448–58; id., in F. Gabrieli (ed.), *L'antica società beduina* (1959), p. 136.

[34] With which one can also compare the Koranic legend of the traveller who falls asleep near a ruined village. He sleeps for a hundred years, and when he awakens the whitened bones of his ass are reunited and covered with flesh by the power of God (Sura ii. 261). Many commentators on the Koran

the Passover sacrifice the bones would not be broken in order that God might restore the victim to life, i.e. ensure the fertility of the flock.

With M. Noth one may also regard this custom as an expression of the communal character of the sacrifice; the wholeness of the victim emphasizes and preserves the cohesion of the family offering it, in which each member is related to the others as bone of their bone, and flesh of their flesh (Gen. ii. 23; 2 Sam. xix. 13 (EVV. 12)).[35] A far simpler explanation has been put forward by R. Dussaud:[36] the prohibition of breaking the bones is intended to enforce the obligation of roasting the victim whole. Not breaking the bones would prevent it being cooked in a pot like a communion sacrifice, or cut in pieces like a holocaust.

The solution remains uncertain, but it is also interesting that outside Israel this custom should be attested above all among nomad peoples, shepherds, or hunters, as Henninger has shown.

5. *The unleavened bread* (Exod. xii. 8)

This is the bread of the Bedouin, made from flour mixed with water and baked like a cake on ashes or on the *sâj*, a heated metal plate. Sometimes Arab nomads eat nothing else besides this,[37] and this bread was the basic food of my Bedouin workmen during the Qumran excavations.

Unleavened loaves admittedly constitute the essential rite of the feast of Unleavened Bread, which is an agricultural feast. But there they have a quite different significance. They are the first loaves made with the new corn, without any element of the previous harvest being mixed with them. This is a symbol of renewal, which is accentuated by the corresponding prescription

connect this legend with Ezra, cf. R. de Vaux and M. J. Steve, *Fouilles à Qaryet el ʿEnab = Abû Gôsh* (1950), pp. 114–15.

35 Cf. M. Noth, *Exodus*² (1959), on xii. 46.

36 R. Dussaud, *Les Origines cananéennes du sacrifice israélite*² (1941), p. 211. J. Henninger, 'Les Fêtes de printemps . . .', considers this explanation too simple. But perhaps his own explanation will be found too far-fetched, namely the application to the Semites—and to the Israelites in particular—of the theory of the 'soul of the bones', attested among the modern nomads of Central Asia.

37 A. Musil, *Arabia Petraea III* (1908), p. 148.

that leavened loaves are to be offered at the feast of Weeks, which closes harvest time and marks the return to normal conditions (Lev. xxiii. 17). However, the rite of unleavened bread, which appears superficially the same at Passover and the feast of Unleavened Bread, could have stimulated the fusion of the two feasts.

6. *The bitter herbs* (Exod. xii. 8; cf. Num. ix. 11)

The Mishnah[38] prescribes five different plants: lettuce, endives, carrots (?), and two kinds of green salad (?). These would signify the bitterness of the sojourn in Egypt.[39] Some modern critics discern an apotropaic power in these herbs,[40] others consider that their function is to ensure the purity of the Passover meal.[41] This is ascribing foreign meanings to what is in fact simply a remnant of nomad custom. These 'bitter herbs' are not garden plants, they are the wild aromatic herbs of the desert, with which the Bedouin season their food.[42] Musil records some half-dozen of these plants which the Rwala Bedouin use.[43] I myself have learned to recognize several of them in the desert of Judah. In 1952, when we were exploring the cliffs of Qumran, we would set out, each of us with a team of Taʿamireh Bedouin, not returning to the camp for lunch. Our Bedouin brought bread and curdled milk or *leben*. At the midday halt they would scatter, and soon return with handfuls of various herbs which seasoned the taste of the bread and went wonderfully well with the *leben*.

7. *The time of sacrifice* (Exod. xii. 6, 10; Num. ix. 3, 5, 11–12)

The victim is immolated 'between the two evenings', i.e. between the disappearance of the sun over the horizon and actual

[38] Pes. ii. 6.

[39] Pes. x. 5. Cf. Deut. xvi. 3: the unleavened bread of the feast of this name is a 'bread of sorrow'.

[40] G. Beer, *Z.A.W.* xxxi (1911), pp. 152–3.

[41] Th. H. Gaster, *Passover. Its History and Traditions* (1949).

[42] Cf. E. Dhorme, *L'Évolution religieuse d'Israël*, 'I. La Religion des Hébreux nomades' (1937), p. 212; J. Henninger, 'Les Fêtes de printemps . . .', p. 420, n. 140.

[43] A. Musil, *The Manners and Customs of the Rwala Bedouins* (1928), p. 95.

nightfall, in other words, during the twilight.[44] It is eaten during the night, and what remains at dawn must be burned. It is the only nocturnal sacrificial meal which is prescribed in the religious law of Israel. Now twilight is the time when the flocks return from their pasture (Gen. xxix. 7), and when the family reassembles for the night; dawn is the time when one sets out once more for the pastures or the moment when one strikes camp to make a fresh stage, leaving nothing behind.[45]

8. *Dress* (Exod. xii. 11)

This is the only sacrifice where a special dress is prescribed. The loins must be girt, sandals on the feet, and staff in the hand. This is the travelling dress, but also that of nomad shepherds. Moses wore sandals when he was shepherding the flocks of Jethro (Exod. iii. 5), and carried a staff (Exod. iv. 2).

11. *The Fixed Date of Passover*

Passover is an annual sacrifice, the date of which is fixed in Exodus xii. 2, 6; Leviticus xxiii. 5; Numbers xxviii. 16; Ezekiel xlv. 21 as the fourteenth day of the first month of the year. These texts refer to the year beginning in spring, in which the first month corresponds to the month of Abib of the ancient calendar (Deut. xvi. 1), and which finally came to be called the month of Nisan, as in Babylonia.[46] In this lunar calendar the fourteenth day coincides with the full moon, and it is still at the full moon of Nisan that the Jews celebrate the Passover.

This date is very ancient. Recently it has been objected that in Deuteronomy xvi. 1 the expression *ḥōḏeš hā-'āḇîḇ* must mean 'the new moon of Abib' on the grounds that up to the Exile the meaning of the word *ḥōḏeš* would have been restricted to 'new moon', and that the term would have been employed in the

[44] *Ancient Israel . . .*, pp. 182–3.
[45] Cf. the expression *hiškîm babbōḳer*, 'strike camp at first light', to signify 'leave early', Judges xix. 8; 1 Sam. xvii. 20, &c.
[46] *Ancient Israel . . .*, pp. 183–6, 191–2.

sense of 'month' only at a later period.[47] This view does not take sufficient account of such early passages as 1 Samuel vi. 1; x. 27, or in the festal calendar itself (Exod. xxiii. 15; xxxiv. 18). A more weighty argument against the celebration of Passover at a fixed date, properly the first full moon of spring, might be taken from one of the Elephantine ostraca. This is a letter which, according to A. Dupont-Sommer, reads: 'Send me word when you celebrate the Passover.'[48] A comparison of this text with the rescript of Darius concerning Passover, likewise found at Elephantine, leads Dupont-Sommer to conclude that at the end of the sixth century B.C., at least in this Jewish colony in Egypt, the date of Passover was not yet precisely determined.[49] However, the uncertainty may bear on another point. The luni-solar calendar requires the periodical intercalation of a supplementary month, a second Adar, which would fall just before Nisan. This intercalation was not subjected to precise rules until much later.[50] Thus one should understand that the author of the letter in question is asking his correspondent whether the Elephantine community is adding a supplementary month that year or not, for this would have the effect of postponing the celebration of Passover by one lunation. The fixing of Passover for the first full moon of spring seems to be as old as the feast itself, and it is this which determined the precise date of the feast of Unleavened Bread when the two feasts were united in the liturgy. The celebration of the feast of Unleavened Bread, an agricultural feast, depended on the state of the harvest, and for a long time its date in the month of Abib, the month of the ripened corn, was only approximate.

Attempts have been made to explain the choice of the full moon for the offering of the Passover sacrifice by connecting it

[47] E. Auerbach, *V.T.* viii (1958), pp. 1 ff. The second part of the verse, where Auerbach himself accepts the sense of 'month', would be a priestly addition.

[48] A. Dupont-Sommer, 'Sur la fête de Pâque dans les documents araméens d'Éléphantine', in *R.E.J.* cvii (1946–7), pp. 39–51. On the same ostracon cf. also E. L. Sukenik and J. Kutscher, in *Kedem* i (1942), pp. 53–56 (in Hebrew).

[49] He is followed by P. Grelot, *V.T.* iv (1954), p. 378, n. 1.

[50] *Ancient Israel* . . ., p. 189.

with astral cults, and by pointing to the predominant role which the lunar divinity would have played among Semitic nomads.[51] Against this opinion, A. Lods has raised the argument that Exodus xii. 22 forbade the people to go out of their houses during the night of Passover, which can hardly be reconciled with a lunar cult.[52] This reply is, however, inadequate since the following verses indicate that the prohibition in question is connected with the tenth plague and with the special circumstances of the Passover in Egypt. The solution is far simpler. As a nocturnal feast of nomad shepherds, Passover was quite naturally celebrated on the night when there was most light, namely that of the full moon.

It is celebrated on the first full moon of spring. This is the season when the animals drop their young and when the milk yield increases.[53] It is also the beginning of the seasonal moving of flocks, the time when the shepherds leave their winter camps to reach the summer grazing grounds in less barren country.[54] It might be objected that in the Passover of Egypt the Israelites do the opposite of this; they leave the cultivated areas to go to the desert. But in the Pentateuch the theme of 'coming out from Egypt' is inseparable from that of entering the Promised Land, and it is natural that the Israelite Passover ritual should be associated with the moment of departure of the people of God for this great change of pastures.[55] The season when sheep and

[51] This is the theory of D. Nielsen, taken up by T. H. Robinson in S. H. Hooke, *Myth and Ritual* (1933), pp. 192–3, and by Oesterley, ibid., p. 118, &c. On the fragility of Nielsen's theory cf. A. Jamme, in *R.B.* lv (1948), pp. 227–44; J. Henninger, 'Sternkunde und Sternkult in Nord- und Zentralarabien', in *Zeitschrift für Ethnologie* lxxix (1954), pp. 82–117.

[52] A. Lods, *Israël, des origines au milieu du viii*[e] *siècle* (1930), p. 339, E.T. by S. H. Hooke (1932), p. 293. Approved by J. Henninger, 'Les Fêtes de printemps . . .', p. 415, n. 116.

[53] References are given by J. Henninger, ibid., p. 395, n. 4.

[54] L. Rost, 'Weidewechsel und altisraelitischer Festkalender', in *Z.D.P.V.* lxvi (1943), pp. 205–16. The connexion which he establishes between the feast of the expiation of the 10th Tishri and the autumn change of pastures is far less evident.

[55] Cf. M. Noth, *Überlieferungsgeschichte des Pentateuch* (1948), pp. 72–73; id., *Exodus*[2] (1959), p. 71. We shall return to this point apropos the historicization of the feast.

goats drop their young, and when this journey to the summer pastures is undertaken, is a dangerous and decisive time for the well-being of the flock. No one knows what dangers await on the road, the state of the pastures themselves, or how one will be welcomed on arrival. It is especially risky for the younger animals. All these dangers are personified in the *Mašḥîṯ*, the Destroyer, mentioned in Exodus xii. 23 (J), and again, in a more abstract and therefore weakened form, in xii. 13 (P). The relation of this Destroyer to Yahweh is left vague.[56] It is a survival of a distant past. It represents the evil forces which threaten the tents and the flocks grouped around them, and it is to guard against these dangers that the 'houses' (originally the tents) are smeared with blood. Perhaps the animals of the flock used also to be smeared with it, as is sometimes done among the Arabs to this day.

III. *Passover Sacrifice and Arab Sacrifices*

We have shown the connexion of the Passover sacrifice with nomadism, and we have emphasized a certain number of features which set it apart from all other Israelite sacrifices. This is the only one which is eaten at night, the only one which requires neither sanctuary nor altar, nor priest (until the Deuteronomist reform), the only one in which the victim is roasted whole and eaten whole without any part being first taken from it as an offering to God. This Passover meal, and the blood ritual which precedes it, are the elements which carry the greatest religious import. They are also the characteristic features of ancient Arab sacrifice.

On this latter point we are relatively ill-informed.[57] Southern

[56] Contrast 2 Sam. xxiv. 16, cf. 1 Chron. xxi. 12, 15, where the Destroyer is identified with the Angel of Yahweh.

[57] The most reliable information is to be found in G. Ryckmans, *Les Religions arabes préislamiques*[3], in M. Gorce and B. Mortier, *Histoire Générale des religions IV* (1960). The work of J. Chelhod, *Le Sacrifice chez les Arabes* (1955), is chiefly concerned with the origins of Islam, and is vitiated by certain over-all views which are disputable. Cf. H. Charles's review in *M.U.B.* xxxii (1955), pp. 222–4, and J. Henninger, 'La Religion bédouine préislamique', in F. Gabrieli (ed.), *L'antica società beduina* (1959), p. 119.

Arabia cannot be cited as evidence, for the texts from this region reflect a sedentary civilization in a fairly advanced stage of evolution.[58] Among the nomads of northern and central Arabia, the sacrificial rites are simple. Each offerer immolates his victim. This is followed by some ritual pouring and sprinkling of the blood. The victim is not burned, but eaten whole by all the participants together.[59]

If one wants to enter into details, one finds hardly any for northern Arabia. The Safaitic inscriptions contain rare allusions to bloody sacrifices. However, there are sixteen inscriptions in which the term *ḏbḥ* is used in connexion with such sacrifices offered by individuals in camping places or near wells, but without any mention of a sanctuary. These sacrifices stem from family forms of cult, and seem to have been somewhat infrequent. Twice they are offered on the occasion of a change of camp.[60] But the term used is interesting. It is the equivalent of the Hebrew word *zeḇaḥ*, which is used for sacrifice of the Passover type, and which was extended to other forms of sacrifice as the ritual became richer and more diverse.[61]

In central Arabia the victims are chosen from the livestock, sheep, cattle, or camels. They are immolated by the offerer, without the intervention of a priest, in front of the idol or divine symbol, which may be no more than a rough stone. The blood is poured over the stone or in the pit which is dug at its foot. No part of the victim is burned on an altar. The flesh is eaten by the sacrificer, his family, and some guests.[62]

[58] J. Henninger has devoted a well-documented article to this point, 'Das Opfer in den altsüdarabischen Hochkulturen', in *Anthropos* xxxviii–xl (1942–5), pp. 779–810. It contains, however, an instructive table of comparisons between southern Arabia on the one hand, and northern and central Arabia on the other.

[59] J. Henninger, 'La Religion bédouine préislamique', pp. 135–6.

[60] G. Ryckmans, 'Le Sacrifice ḎBḤ dans les inscriptions safaïtiques', in *H.U.C.A.* xxviii. 1 (1950–1), pp. 431–8.

[61] *zeḇaḥ* designates a sacrifice in which an animal victim is immolated (as opposed to cereal offerings), and eaten (as opposed to holocausts). These are the features which chiefly characterize both the Passover sacrifice and the communion sacrifice, *šᵉlāmîm*. The communion sacrifice seems to have been practised by the Israelites only after the settlement, cf. p. 20 and n. 74.

[62] G. Ryckmans, *Les Religions arabes préislamiques*[3], p. 203.

These similarities are all the more significant in view of the fact that the features which the Passover sacrifice and the Arab form of sacrifice have in common are precisely those which distinguish both forms from other types of Israelite sacrifice and other sacrificial rituals of the Ancient East, especially from Canaanite ritual.

Passover shows particular affinities with the feasts which the Arabs celebrated in the first month of spring, the month of Rajab. Victims were sacrificed and eaten at this time to ensure the fertility and prosperity of the flock. This parallel had already been pointed out by Ewald more than a century ago.[63] Recently it has been recalled by J. Henninger,[64] who has extended the comparison to the pastoral peoples of central and northern Asia. This author interprets the sacrifice in question as an offering of the first-born of the flock, and ascribes the same significance to the Israelite Passover. But his argument is unconvincing and, as I have already said, Passover did not have this character.[65]

The similarities between the Passover sacrifice and the ancient Arab sacrifices, especially those of the month of Rajab, are too close to be accidental. They bear witness to a common origin, and they determine the primitive character of Passover. It is a sacrifice of nomad or semi-nomad shepherds, offered for the good of the flock in spring, when goats and sheep drop their young, and when the journey to the summer pastures is undertaken.

This primitive character makes it certain that the rite is anterior to settled life, and its antiquity in this respect is probably responsible for the obscurity which surrounds the name by

[63] H. Ewald, *Zeitschrift für die Kunde des Morgenlandes* iii (1840), pp. 410–41; taken up by Wellhausen, Robertson Smith, &c., especially by M.-J. Lagrange, *Études sur les religions sémitiques*[2] (1905), pp. 256 and 298–9.

[64] In 'Les Fêtes de printemps . . .'.

[65] The only argument which carries any weight is drawn from philology. The sacrifice of Rajab is called *'atîra*, which designates both the rite and the victim (like *pesaḥ* in Hebrew) and which is defined by the *Lisân*: 'first-born animal sacrificed to the gods'. But traditionists distinguish between *'atîra* and *fara'*, 'first-born'; cf. W. Robertson Smith, *Lectures on the Religion of the Semites*[2] (1894), p. 228 note.

which it is designated. No satisfactory explanation has yet been given of the word *pesaḥ*.[66] Recourse should not be had to Akkadian[67] or Egyptian[68] etymologies, since the rite is unknown in Mesopotamia and Egypt. In the account of Exodus xii the word is explained as a derivative of the verb *psḥ*, the strict meaning of which in Hebrew is 'to be crippled, to limp, to hop', and which acquires the secondary and derived meaning of 'leaping over, passing beyond, sparing'. Yahweh has 'spared' the houses marked with the blood of the Passover victim.[69] However, it is difficult to accept this explanation as correct, for it is semantically forced and is, moreover, connected with the special circumstances of the Passover of Egypt. Certain modern authors rely on the use of the verb *psḥ* in a ritual sense in 1 Kings xviii. 26, and envisage a sort of dance which would originally have accompanied the sacrifice. Unfortunately the texts have nothing to say of this. It is better to recognize our ignorance.

The biblical texts themselves presuppose that Passover was already celebrated prior to the Exodus from Egypt. In order to obtain Pharaoh's permission to leave, Moses and the Israelites insist that they must go to the desert 'to sacrifice to Yahweh' (Exod. iii. 18; v. 3; viii. 4, 17, 21–24 (EVV. 8, 21, 25–28)), 'to render worship to him' (Exod. iv. 23; vii. 16, 26 (EVV. viii. 1); viii. 16 (EVV. 20); ix. 1, 13; x. 3, 7, 11, 24, 26), 'to celebrate a feast in honour of Yahweh' (Exod. v. 1). It is reasonable to suppose that Passover is referred to.[70] According to Exodus viii. 22 (EVV. 26) the victims for these intended sacrifices would be animals the sacrificing of which the Egyptians would declare sacrilegious. The cult of the ram, which was widespread in the

[66] Cf. L. Koehler and W. Baumgartner, *Lexicon in Veteris Testamenti Libros*[2] (1958), s.v., 'etymologisch noch nicht befriedigend gedeuteter'.

[67] H. Zimmern, *Die Keilschriften und das Alte Testament* (1903), p. 610.

[68] F. Hommel, *Die altisraelitische Überlieferung in inschriftlicher Beleuchtung* (1897), p. 293; B. Couroyer, *R.B.* lxii (1955), pp. 481–96.

[69] Exod. xii. 13, 23, 27. This sense occurs elsewhere only in Isa. xxxi. 5, which most probably depends on Exodus, or on the tradition which this represents.

[70] A difficulty occurs only in a single passage: Exod. x. 25 speaks of *zᵉḇāḥîm* and holocausts. This may be a redactional alteration.

Delta,[71] should be remembered. On the other hand, the Yahwist passage relating to the Passover, which follows immediately upon the statement of the death of the Egyptian first-born in the same tradition (Exod. xi. 1–6), begins without explanation with the words: 'Go . . . and sacrifice the Passover' (Exod. xii. 21). This passage, and also the priestly passage of Exodus xii. 11, seem to indicate that we are dealing with a pre-existing rite, which is here prescribed for this particular situation.

It may even be asked whether the Passover type of sacrifice was not the only form of sacrifice which the Israelites knew up to the time of their final settlement in Canaan. At all events, the Bible is extremely reticent with regard to other sacrifices. In Exodus xviii. 12 a holocaust and *zᵉḇāḥîm* are offered, but they are offered by Jethro, who is not an Israelite. The same remark applies, and with still greater force, to the holocausts of Balak, who is the king of Moab (Num. xxiii). In Exodus xxxii. 6, 8, the Israelites themselves offer holocausts and *šᵉlāmîm*, communion sacrifices. But these sacrifices are condemned, because they are offered to the golden calf in a form of worship copied from the Canaanites. In Exodus xx. 24 holocausts and *šᵉlāmîm* are mentioned in connexion with the law of the altar, with which the Book of the Covenant opens, and in Exodus xxiv. 5 holocausts and *šᵉlāmîm* are offered at the conclusion of the covenant, the official document of which is the Book of the Covenant, referred to in verse 7. In the final compilation of the Pentateuch, this Book of the Covenant is attached to the events of Sinai, but there are good reasons for supposing that it is later than the settlement, and that it represents the law of the tribal confederation in connexion with the pact of Shechem.[72] If this explanation is found unsatisfactory, it should at least be conceded that the redactors of traditions relating to the desert could have been describing the sacrifices offered by their ancestors in the form current at the epoch in which they were writing. Two texts from the

[71] Cf. B. Couroyer, *L'Exode*² (1958), *in loco*; H. Bonnet, *Reallexikon d. ägyptischen Religionsgeschichte* (1952), s.v. 'Widder'.

[72] Cf. *Ancient Israel . . .*, p. 143.

prophets may perhaps be cited. Amos v. 25 and Jeremiah vii. 22 say that the Israelites in the desert offered neither *zᵉḇāḥîm* nor cereal oblations, since God had given them no mandate for holocaust or *zeḇaḥ*. Absolutely speaking, it might be said that these prophets condemn only the formalized cult practised by their contemporaries.[73] But if *zeḇaḥ* is taken in the sense of 'communion sacrifice', a synonym for *šᵉlāmîm*, a sense which is frequent elsewhere, then a clear reflection can be found in these passages of the fact that the Israelites in the desert were not yet acquainted with holocausts and communion sacrifices.[74]

IV. *Passover and the Exodus from Egypt*

Whatever one concludes on this last point, it is certain that the Passover sacrifice is a very ancient ritual, going back to Israel's nomadic period, and practised by the ancestors of the Israelites and by other pastoral Semites. But in Israel this ritual acquired a special significance. In the account of Exodus xii, in the Yahwist version no less than in the priestly one, Passover is connected with the Exodus from Egypt. It is the 'memorial' of this event (Exod. xii. 14), and such is the meaning of it, of which succeeding generations of the people must be reminded from age to age (Exod. xii. 26–27): that night Yahweh spared the houses marked with the blood of the Passover victim. The connexion with history is thus achieved by the medium of the blood rite, which, in the primitive and pre-Israelite form of Passover, already had an apotropaic force, and which now protects the Israelites from the tenth plague, the death of the first-born in Egypt. It is an act of salvation wrought by Yahweh. But the

[73] This is what I myself wrote in *Ancient Israel . . .*, p. 428.

[74] The type of sacrifice known as the *šᵉlāmîm*, the communion sacrifice, is not found among the ancient Arabs, nor in Mesopotamia or Egypt, but the Israelites hold it in common with the Canaanites, Moabites, Ammonites . . . and the Greeks, where it is represented by the *θυσία*. Is it not reasonable to conclude that it was a pre-Semitic and pre-Hellenic rite of the Eastern Mediterranean basin, adopted by the Canaanites and transmitted by them to the Israelites after their installation in Canaan? See Chap. II.

passage does not express any connexion between the first-born of the Egyptians and the first-born of the flock which, according to some, would have been offered on the occasion of Passover. We have already explained our position with regard to this false interpretation of Passover.[75]

This annual festival, unique in character, served therefore to commemorate a unique event in the history of Israel. In one particular spring, at the time when sacrifices were offered to ensure the good of the flock and to mark the departure for the summer pastures, Yahweh saved the people by a stupendous intervention, and led them out of Egypt finally to install them in the Promised Land.[76] This does not mean that the account in Exodus xii is simply a 'cultic legend' without any perceptible connexion with history.[77] On the contrary, it means that the cult has preserved the memory of one of the most important stages in the history of Salvation. Unlike other ancient religions, the religion of Israel is an 'historical' religion.[78]

This 'historicization' of Passover must have taken place very early. After the settlement, the significance of this nomadic sacrifice was inevitably obscured. The rite is preserved, but it has been charged with a new meaning. The connexion with the history of Salvation already existed, as we have seen, in the Yahwist tradition, and it is very probably earlier than it. As a result, a new interpretation of the rites emerged. The name *pesaḥ* was explained by Yahweh's act of 'leaping over' the houses marked with the blood of the victim. The Destroyer, the *Mašḥîṯ*, became the inflictor of the plague unleashed by Yahweh against the Egyptians (Exod. xii. 13 (P), 23 (J)). The nomadic dress and the unleavened bread became the symbol of the urgency and haste of the departure (Exod. xii. 11, 39).

[75] Cf. pp. 6 and 17, with n. 65.

[76] Cf. M. Noth, *Überlieferungsgeschichte des Pentateuch* (1948), pp. 72–73.

[77] Against J. Pedersen, *Z.A.W.* lii (1934), pp. 161–75, and *Israel: Its Life and Culture III–IV* (1940), 2nd ed. (1959), Appendix I.

[78] Cf. S. Mowinckel, 'Die vermeintliche "Passahlegende" . . .', in *Studia Theologica* v (1952), pp. 66–88.

v. *Passover and the Feast of Unleavened Bread*

Corresponding to the feast of the flocks celebrated by the shepherds in the spring, the peasants had another feast falling at the same time of year: the feast of the first-fruits of the harvest. Among the settled Israelites this sacred time lasted from the beginning of the barley harvest to the end of the wheat harvest, and it was framed between the feast of Unleavened Bread, *maṣṣôṯ*, and the feast of Weeks, seven weeks after the feast of Unleavened Bread. This feast of first-fruits celebrated the renewal of agricultural life, and, as an indication of this, for seven days unleavened loaves or *maṣṣôṯ* were eaten, unmixed with any element from the previous harvest. Inversely, at the feast of Weeks, which brought this period to a close, the ritual prescribed the unusual oblation of leavened loaves, signifying the return to ordinary conditions.[79]

This peasant feast of *maṣṣôṯ* was observed only after the entry into Canaan,[80] and it is probable that it was borrowed from the Canaanites. But given that the feast of *maṣṣôṯ*, which extended from Sabbath to Sabbath, is incorporated in the time system based on the week (Exod. xii. 16; Deut. xvi. 8; Lev. xxiii. 6–8), and that the week and the Sabbath are not attested outside Israel,[81] it can be concluded that this feast assumed, apparently from the time of its adoption, a specifically Israelite character.

In the ancient calendars of Exodus xxiii and xxxiv, it is one of the three great annual festivals which involved a pilgrimage to the sanctuary. Very early too in these calendars (Exod. xxiii. 15 and xxxiv. 18), as in the Yahwist tradition in Exodus xii. 23–27, 39, it was connected with the history of Salvation, and specifically with the same event which was commemorated in Passover: the Exodus from Egypt.[82]

79 The rabbis call the feast of Weeks *'aṣereṯ*, 'Concluding assembly', and even ' *'aṣereṯ* of Passover'.

80 Cf. Lev. xxiii. 10 on the offering of the first sheaf, and Deut. xxvi. 1–2 on the first-fruits of the earth.

81 Cf. *Ancient Israel* . . ., pp. 186–8, 475–80.

82 Add Deut. xvi. 3: the *maṣṣôṯ* are a 'bread of sorrow' which recalls the haste with which the people left Egypt.

It is natural that throughout the period of the monarchy this agricultural feast and annual pilgrimage to the central sanctuary should have eclipsed Passover, which was a shepherds' feast. However, the latter continued to be celebrated as a family feast, chiefly perhaps in those districts in which pastoral traditions were best preserved, i.e. in Judah. In fact the first sure mention of Passover in the historical books is in 2 Kings xxiii. 21–23, where Josiah has the Passover celebrated at Jerusalem in accordance with the prescriptions of Deuteronomy, which imposed the obligation of coming to the single sanctuary to immolate the Passover victim (Deut. xvi. 2). This reform, the result of the law of the single place of cult (Deut. xii), is indisputable proof that the Passover had continued to be observed since the settlement, but away from the central sanctuary.[83]

We have said that in the primitive form of Deuteronomy Passover was not yet combined with the feast of Unleavened Bread. However, after the Deuteronomist reform, this fusion became inevitable. In effect, the religious law thenceforward imposed the same obligation of coming to the Temple for Passover and the feast of Unleavened Bread alike, and at the same time, namely in the spring. Moreover, the two feasts had a rite in common, that of unleavened bread, which was the principal element of the feast of this name and an accessory element in the feast of Passover. Finally, the two feasts had long been connected with the same event in the history of Salvation, the Exodus from Egypt. It is the date of Passover, fixed right from the first as the full moon of the first month in spring, which determined the date, hitherto imprecise, of the feast of Unleavened Bread and, as a consequence, the date of the feast of Weeks.

If one admits that the Holiness Code, in which the two feasts are combined (Lev. xxiii. 5–8), is a law of the Jerusalem Temple, codified a little before the Exile, it follows that this fusion of Passover with the feast of Unleavened Bread was achieved after Josiah but still before the Exile. Ezekiel xlv. 21

[83] Against certain authors, and recently J. G. Février, in *J.A.* ccxlviii (1960), pp. 184–5.

merely takes up this arrangement in the Holiness Code. It is this which determined the liturgy of the Second Temple (Num. xxviii. 16–25, cf. Ezra vi. 19–22) and which continues to regulate the Jewish cult. Passover was celebrated on the 14th day of Nisan and the feast of Unleavened Bread, which was no longer tied to a Sabbath, began on the 15th day.

VI. *Religious Significance of Passover*

All this historical evolution must be taken into account in order to discover the religious significance of the Passover sacrifice: after the settlement, Passover and the feast of Unleavened Bread commemorated the liberation of the people coming out of Egypt under Yahweh's guidance. Passover was a 'memorial', *zikkārôn* (Exod. xii. 14), as also was the feast of Unleavened Bread (Exod. xiii. 9). But the liturgy actualizes this memorial of the past and makes it a present event. In explaining Passover to his son the Israelite had to say: 'It is because of what Yahweh did for *me*, when *I* came out of Egypt' (Exod. xiii. 8), and the Mishnah develops this aspect at the end of the tractate on Passover: 'It is because we have the duty of thanking, honouring, praising, magnifying, exalting, and elevating Him who performed all these wonders upon *us* and upon our fathers, and who brought *us* from slavery into liberty.'[84]

Passover also acquired a messianic significance which was intensified in the period immediately preceding our era. A memorial of the past, an assurance of present salvation, Passover finally expressed the hope of salvation to come. Just as in Egypt Passover had been 'a night of watching for Yahweh' (Exod. xii. 42) so in later times it was celebrated in the expectation of a new visitation by God.[85] After the destruction of the Temple, Rabbi Aqiba composed this paschal prayer: 'So may Yahweh our God and the God of our fathers bring us in peace to other set feasts which are coming to meet us.'[86]

[84] Pes. x. 5.

[85] I. Zolli, *Il Nazareno* (1938), p. 213; P. Strobel, in *Z.N.W.* xlix (1958), pp. 157–96, especially 164–71.

[86] Pes. x. 6.

Passover therefore has become a sacrament of the Old Covenant, which conforms to St. Thomas Aquinas' definition of a sacrament: a sign which commemorates a past fact, manifests a present effect, and announces a future good. Because he is speaking of the sacraments of the New Covenant, St. Thomas defines them in relation to their common cause, which manifests all its power in *the* sacrament *par excellence*, the Eucharist, towards which all the other sacraments are ordered. The complete text runs as follows: 'A sacrament is therefore a sign which simultaneously calls to mind the past cause, the Passion of Christ, manifests the effect of this Passion in us, namely grace, and announces the glory of the future.'[87]

This is the justification which theology can offer of the typological sense attributed to the Old Testament Passover in several passages of the New Testament. However, one text which is often quoted must be set aside, namely John i. 29: 'Behold the Lamb of God who takes away the sins of the world.' The reference is not to the Passover victim but to the Servant of Yahweh of Isaiah liii, who is 'like a lamb led to the slaughter' on whom 'Yahweh has laid the crimes of us all', who was 'struck dead for our sins . . . and by his stripes we are healed'. On the other hand the following passage in St. Paul must be given its full force: 'For Christ your Passover is sacrificed. Let us therefore celebrate the feast . . . with the unleavened bread of purity and truth' (1 Cor. v. 7–8). Recalling that the bones of Christ dead on the Cross were not broken, John xix. 36 recognizes in this the fulfilment of the image expressed in one of the Passover rites which, as we have explained, provides a symbol of survival and salvation. This typology of the New Testament is very restrained, but it provides a basis and an authentication for the developments given to it by the Fathers and in the paschal liturgy of Holy Week, where the texts of the Exodus here commented upon are employed. Christ, the Victim of the New Covenant, is sacrificed on the Cross and eaten at the Last Supper, in the context of the Jewish Passover, which has become our Holy

[87] *Summa Theologica* III, qu. lx, art. 3.

Week. But, as with all typology, as in every transition from the Old to the New Covenant, the reality surpasses all that the type prefigures. The Passion of Christ and its 'memorial', the Eucharist, are not a continuation of the Old Testament Passover. They constitute a new Passover.[88]

[88] I have been unable to take account of J. B. Segal, *The Hebrew Passover from the Earliest Times to A.D. 70* (1963), which appeared when these lectures were already in the press. The book is valuable for its full documentation, which includes the Mishnah and the customs of the Samaritans; but I cannot agree with the author's main conclusions. Segal denies that the Passover was originally a nomadic sacrifice which was independent of *maṣṣôṯ*, and he explains Passover and *maṣṣôṯ* as a spring New Year festival. This is quite contrary to the argument advanced in the foregoing pages, and the reading of his book leaves me unconvinced of any need to change my point of view.

II

HOLOCAUSTS AND COMMUNION SACRIFICES

THE two most frequently attested kinds of sacrifice in the Old Testament, which are also the most characteristic of Israelite ritual, are the holocaust, *'ôlāh*, and the communion sacrifice, *šᵉlāmîm*. When we have described and explained the final form of the ritual which regulated the offering of these sacrifices, we shall retrace their historical development. Then we shall deduce their significance, and finally we shall attempt to determine their origin.

I. *The Ritual of the Holocaust and the Communion Sacrifice*

1. *The holocaust*

The name of holocaust, *'ôlāh*, is ordinarily[1] explained by the root *'ālāh*, 'to ascend'. It is the sacrifice in which the victim 'ascends' to the altar, or, perhaps better, the smoke of which 'ascends' to God.[2] Its characteristic feature is, in fact, that the entire victim is carried on to the altar, without any part being given back to the offerer, or priest (except the skin), and that the whole victim is burned.

The most complete ritual of this form of sacrifice, like that of the *šᵉlāmîm*, is found in the sacrificial code of Leviticus i–vii, which belongs to the latest redaction of the Pentateuch, and which describes the ceremonies of the Second Temple; but the principal rites are certainly more ancient.

1 And by the Bible itself, cf. the very frequent use of the verb in the expression 'to make the *'ôlāh* to ascend'.

2 Cf. G. B. Gray, *Sacrifice in the Old Testament: Its Theory and Practice* (1925), p. 7; W. O. E. Oesterley, *Sacrifices in Ancient Israel* (1937), p. 85.

According to Leviticus i, the victim is a male without blemish, either from the cattle or sheep, as the Holiness Code had already prescribed (Lev. xxii. 18–20). According to Leviticus i. 14 ff., a bird may also be offered, but only a turtle-dove or a pigeon. The parallel ritual of the sacrifice for sin (Lev. v. 7, cf. xii. 8) indicates that these animals were accepted as the offerings of the poor, and their omission in the Holiness Code suggests that they constitute an addition to the ancient ritual. The victim is presented by the offerer himself, who places his hand on its head. This gesture has been interpreted in different ways.[3] It cannot be explained as a magic rite 'intended to penetrate the animal with the soul of the sacrificer'.[4] Nor is it, as is often contended, a symbol of the substitution of the victim for the offerer, whose sins it assumes in order to expiate them.[5] It is true that, in the ceremony of the scapegoat (Lev. xvi. 21), the same gesture is used to lay the sins of the people on the animal. But precisely as a result of this transference, the goat becomes impure, and is driven off into the desert instead of being sacrificed. The sacrificial victims, on the contrary, are holy. However, the gesture does signify more than an abandonment of proprietary rights over the victim, such as the *manumissio* of Roman law. In placing his hand on the animal's head, the offerer attests that this victim is *his* indeed, that the sacrifice which is about to be presented by the priest is offered in *his* name, and that the benefits accruing from it will return to *him*.[6]

[3] Cf. P. Volz's old study, 'Die Handauflegung beim Opfer', *Z.A.W.* xxi (1901), pp. 93–100, and the recent discussion by E. Lohse, *Die Ordination im Spätjudentum und im Neuen Testament* (1951), pp. 23–25.

[4] R. Dussaud, *Les Origines cananéennes du sacrifice israélite*^{2} (1941), p. 72.

[5] It is true that Lev. i. 4 gives expression to the expiatory force of the holocaust in the same passage in which it records this gesture, but according to the doctrine of Leviticus this expiatory force is attached not to the gesture of the imposition of hands, but to the blood rite (cf. Lev. xvii. 11). Furthermore, it is significant that when the same gesture is mentioned in connexion with sacrifices for sin (Lev. iv. 4, &c.), no expression of this idea is attached to it. On the subject of reparation sacrifices the imposition of hands is not even mentioned (Lev. v. 15 ff.).

[6] Cf. E. Lohse, loc. cit.; W. Eichrodt, *Theologie des Alten Testaments I*^{6} (1959), p. 101, with notes 341 and 342; H. Wheeler Robinson, in *J.T.S.* xliii

The offerer himself cuts the victim's throat some distance from the altar (Lev. i. 5); it is he also who skins the victim, cuts it into pieces, and washes the entrails and feet (Lev. i. 6, 9). This is what Leviticus prescribes. However, according to Ezekiel xliv. 11, the actual slaughter is the task of the Levites, while in 2 Chronicles xxix. 22, 24, the victims are sacrificed by the priests, and cut up by the priests assisted by the Levites according to 2 Chronicles xxix. 34, by the Levites according to 2 Chronicles xxxv. 11.[7] Possibly the practice wavered after the return from the Exile,[8] but the ancient custom canonized by the priestly code prevailed, and the laity retained the privilege of slaughtering their own victims up to the end of the Second Temple.[9]

The part of the priest, then, begins when the victim comes in contact with the altar. It is he who pours the blood around the altar (Lev. i. 5), and he who places the quarters of flesh on the altar, together with the head, the fat, the entrails, and the feet (Lev. i. 8–9). The role of priest and altar here must be emphasized. It was not apparent in the Passover sacrifice, and in other forms of sacrifice it did not appear at once as an indispensable necessity. But in the Israelite ritual as finally constituted, and even for the Passover sacrifice from Deuteronomy onwards, sacrifice, priest, and altar are necessarily connected to each other. Without priest and altar no sacrifice can be legitimate, and the priest is the exclusive minister of the altar (1 Sam. ii. 28; 2 Kings xxiii. 9; cf. Deut. xxxiii. 10; 2 Chron. xxvi. 16–18).

Except for the skin, which is the priest's perquisite (Lev. vii. 8), everything is carried on to the altar, where a fire burns ceaselessly (Lev. vi. 5–6), and everything is burned.[10]

(1942), p. 131: 'By placing (the hands) on the animal the offerer says intensively: "This is mine, and it is I who offer it".'

[7] On these passages cf. J. Hänel, 'Das Recht des Opferschlachtens in der chronistischen Literatur', in *Z.A.W.* lv (1937), pp. 46–67. In Leviticus itself the Samaritan text, and still more often the Septuagint, have the plural instead of the singular, thus ascribing the action to the priests rather than to the offerer.

[8] Concerning the Passover sacrifice cf. J. Jeremias, *Die Passahfeier der Samaritaner* (Beihefte zur *Z.A.W.* 59) (1932), pp. 86–87.

[9] Cf. Mishnah, Zebaḥim, iii. 1.

[10] The instruction on the lighting of the fire in Lev. i. 7 applies only to the first sacrifice, which is considered to follow the promulgation of the law.

When the victim is a bird (Lev. i. 14–17) the ritual is correspondingly modified. There is no imposition of hands or slaughtering. All is carried out at the altar itself, and for that reason it is carried out by the priest in person. He wrings off its head and lets the blood flow down the side of the altar. He plucks the bird, divides it in two, and burns it.

According to the additional rubric of Numbers xv. 1–16, both the holocaust and the communion sacrifice are accompanied by a cereal offering, *minḥāh*,[11] of the finest ground flour with oil, and a libation of wine. The same prescription applies to the daily holocaust (Exod. xxix. 38–42; Num. xxviii. 4–8), to the holocaust offered at the presentation of the first sheaf (Lev. xxiii. 13), and to the holocausts of the feast of Weeks (Lev. xxiii. 18). In the absence of any indication to the contrary, it may be supposed that the ordinary rite for cereal offerings was followed (Lev. ii). The offering went to the priests, except for a handful which was burned on the altar as an *'azkārāh*. The exact sense of this term is disputed. Either it is a 'memorial' which recalls the offerer to the mind of God, or—and perhaps this is nearer to the sense—it is a 'pledge' which recalls that the offering is to be considered as a whole, of which God accepts this part as representative.[12]

In this ritual of Leviticus i we are confronted from the outset with the fluidity of the vocabulary relating to sacrifices.[13] The holocaust is here called a *ḳorbān* (Lev. i. 2, 10, 14), something which one 'brings near' to God or to the altar. In Leviticus and Numbers this term is very frequent, but outside them it is found only in Ezekiel xx. 28 and xl. 43 (text uncertain). It applies to all sacrifices, even to non-sacrificial offerings, and it is a creation of the priestly code. In this same chapter the holocaust is also called *'iššeh* (Lev. i. 9, 13, 17). This word appears first in passages due to Deuteronomist redaction (Deut. xviii. 1; Joshua

[11] On the sense of *minḥāh* cf. N. H. Snaith, *V.T.* vii (1957), pp. 314–16.

[12] Cf. G. R. Driver, *J.S.S.* i (1956), pp. 99–100.

[13] On this vocabulary cf. G. B. Gray, op. cit., pp. 3–20; W. O. E. Oesterley, op. cit., pp. 75–94; L. Moraldi, 'Terminologia cultuale israelitica', in *Rivista degli Studi Orientali* xxxii (1957) (*Scritti in onore di G. Furlani*), pp. 321–37.

xiii. 14; 1 Sam. ii. 28), and it is conjecturally restored in 1 Kings ix. 15. It is frequent in the priestly writings, and it reappears in ben Sirach (Hebr.) xlv. 21; l. 13. The etymology and the original sense are disputed,[14] but it seems certain that the priestly writers connect it with *'ēš*, 'fire', and that by it they understand all offerings consumed wholly or in part by fire. A more ancient term is *kālîl*, but its force is uncertain. The root expresses the idea of totality and integrity. It is in apposition to *'ôlāh* in 1 Samuel vii. 9, it seems to mean 'holocaust' in Deuteronomy xxxiii. 10, but *kālîl* is mentioned together with *'ôlāh* in Psalms li. 21 (EVV. 19), which shows that the two words were not exactly synonyms. The Carthaginians knew of a sacrifice called *šlm kll*, which may be the holocaust, and also a *kll* sacrifice which is different from it.[15]

2. *The communion sacrifice*

This is how we translate the sacrifice known as *zeḇaḥ šᵉlāmîm* in the priestly rituals. Elsewhere the two terms rarely occur together. More often one finds *zeḇaḥ* alone, or *šᵉlāmîm* alone. We shall discuss the sense of these different terms and their interrelationship in the course of examining the significance of this form of sacrifice. Its characteristic feature is that the victim is immolated, and that it is shared between God, the priest, and the offerer.[16] The ritual is contained in Leviticus iii, to which must be added Leviticus vii. 11–38 for the different forms which this sacrifice can assume and for the portion which goes to the

[14] H. Cazelles is responsible for the last hypothesis, *Le Lévitique*² (1958), p. 13; id., *Le Deutéronome*² (1958), p. 82, n. *e*: the word, he contends, comes from the Sumerian EŠ and designates the 'food' offered to Yahweh. This opinion is very difficult to justify.

[15] Cf. below, p. 45. It is generally admitted that the word passed into Egyptian in the form *krr*, and appeared in that language at the end of the New Empire, Erman–Grapow, *Wörterbuch der Ägyptischen Sprache*, v. 61. But the holocaust is unknown or extremely rare in Egyptian religion, cf. R. Dussaud, *Les Origines cananéennes du sacrifice israélite*, pp. 159 ff.

[16] Apart from the general works already cited, cf. W. B. Stevenson, 'Hebrew 'Olah and Zebach Sacrifices', in *Festschrift für A. Bertholet* (1950), pp. 488–97; N. H. Snaith, 'Sacrifices in the Old Testament', in *V.T.* vii (1957), pp. 308–14.

priests, Leviticus x. 14–15 again for the priests' portion, and Leviticus xxii. 21–24 for the choice of victims.

The victim is an animal from the cattle or small livestock which can be male or female, while the holocaust requires a male. Again, in contrast to the holocaust, birds are not accepted. The beginning of the ritual is the same as for the holocaust. The victim is presented by the offerer, who lays his hand upon it and slaughters it himself. The priest pours out the blood around the altar.

One part of the victim is burned on the altar as an *'iššeh* (cf. under holocaust) for Yahweh. This includes all the fat which surrounds the entrails, the two kidneys, and the fat tail in the case of sheep. The reason is that the fat, like the blood, belongs to Yahweh. 'All fat belongs to Yahweh. . . . You shall eat neither fat nor blood' (Lev. iii. 16–17; cf. vii. 23–25).

In the recent forms of the ritual the breast and the right thigh are assigned to the priests (Lev. vii. 28–34; x. 14–15). The apportionment of the breast is called a *t^enûp̱āh*, that of the thigh a *t^erûmāh*. The second term involves no difficulty. It is a 'levy' taken by the priests. The first term is generally translated 'waving'; the breast would first be 'waved' before Yahweh before being handed over to the priest.[17] But the same term is used in connexion with the consecration of the Levites (Num. viii. 11, 13, 15) and clearly they are not 'waved' before Yahweh; the two terms are, moreover, used indiscriminately in various contexts (so in Exod. xxxv. 1–9 and 22) and in Numbers xviii. 11 they are synonyms. It is probable that the two words are influenced by the juridical language of Mesopotamia, and that *t^erûmāh* and *t^enûp̱āh* signify respectively 'levy' and 'contribution'.[18]

The offerer receives the rest of the flesh, which he eats with his family and with any guests he may invite, provided that they

[17] A. Vincent, 'Les Rites du balancement (tenoûphah) et du prélèvement (teroûmah) dans le sacrifice de communion de l'Ancien Testament', in *Mélanges Syriens offerts à R. Dussaud I* (1939), pp. 267–72.

[18] G. R. Driver, 'Three Technical Terms in the Pentateuch', in *J.S.S.* i (1956), pp. 97–105.

are in a state of ritual purity. The meat is not roasted, as in the Passover sacrifice, but cooked in a pot, cf. Leviticus viii. 31 and Exodus xxix. 31; Numbers vi. 19; cf. the temple kitchens in Ezekiel xlvi. 24,[19] and the accounts in Judges vi. 19; 1 Samuel ii. 13–14.

The rituals of Leviticus vii. 12–17 and xxii. 21–23, 29–30, distinguish three kinds of communion sacrifice: the sacrifice of praise, *tôḏāh*, offered on the occasion of a solemnity,[20] the free-will sacrifice, *n^eḏāḇāh*, offered out of devotion apart from any prescription or promise, and the votive sacrifice, *neḏer*, which the offerer is bound by vow to perform. The *tôḏāh* sacrifice has to be consumed the same day, the *n^eḏāḇāh* and *neḏer* may be kept until the day following, but what remains over to the third day has to be burned. The rules are recent and remain imprecise. Numbers xv. 1–12, cf. Leviticus xxii. 18–20, applies the same distinctions to holocausts with reference to the cereal offerings which accompany them. These names indicate the motives or occasions of sacrifices rather than the different kinds. According to Leviticus vii. 12–14 the *tôḏāh* sacrifice is completed by an offering of unleavened cakes and leavened bread: one of these cakes is levied for Yahweh and this is handed over to the priest.

According to Numbers xv. 1–12 all the forms of sacrifice are accompanied by an offering of finely ground flour mixed with oil, together with a libation of wine. Here too a certain imprecision in the terminology and a certain confusion between the rituals should be noted.

II. *Historical Development*

Apart from the daily service in the Temple and the ritual of the great feasts—points to which we shall return—the holocaust is rarely mentioned in ancient texts. Isaac was to be offered as

[19] Cf. A. Lods, 'Les Cuisines du Temple de Jérusalem', in *R.H.R.* cxxvii (1944—A), pp. 30–54.

[20] This conclusion may legitimately be drawn from the parallelism with Num. xv. 3.

a holocaust, and it was as this form of sacrifice that the ram substituted for him was offered (Gen. xxii). Jephthah's daughter was offered as a holocaust (Judges xi. 31). Under the Judges, too, Gideon offered a holocaust (Judges vi. 26, 28); the second tradition on Gideon (Judges vi. 18–22) is less clear, but it seems that the meal Gideon wishes to offer to the Angel of Yahweh in hospitality is changed into a holocaust by the fire springing up from the rock. We have an analogous, but more explicit, account for the holocaust of Manoah, the father of Samson (Judges xiii. 15–20). Later evidence for holocausts offered alone are: the holocaust offered when the ark is handed over by the Philistines (1 Sam. vi. 14), Samuel's holocausts (1 Sam. vii. 9), and Saul's (1 Sam. xiii. 10, 12) (but cf. verse 9 and x. 8), then Solomon's (1 Kings iii. 4), and later, outside Jerusalem, the sacrifice of Elijah on Carmel (1 Kings xviii. 38). Elsewhere the holocaust is joined to the communion sacrifice. In short, the holocaust is offered alone only in exceptional circumstances.

As in Leviticus, the victims are domestic animals, cattle, or small livestock.[21] The sacrifice of birds is never mentioned in the historical texts. The characteristic feature is the same: all is burned on the altar. Apart from the sacrifices of Gideon and Manoah, the unique nature of which prevents us from drawing any conclusion, we have very few details as to the nature of the rites which were observed. Certain differences from later ritual may, however, be noticed. The immolation of Isaac was intended to take place actually *on* the altar where the wood had been arranged (Gen. xxii. 9). Possibly the holocaust of 1 Samuel vi. 14 should be represented in the same way, and the episode of 1 Samuel xiv. 32–35 is easier to understand if the victim of the holocaust and those of the communion sacrifice were immolated on the altar. By contrast in the sacrifice of Carmel the bull is slaughtered and cut up before being set on the wood of the altar (1 Kings xviii. 23, 33).

In ancient times the communion sacrifice was the most frequent, and it is mentioned forty-seven times in the historical

[21] Except for the human sacrifice of Jephthah's daughter, cf. p. 65.

books, from Joshua to Kings. It is offered on the great feasts, on the occasion of a pilgrimage to the sanctuary (1 Sam. i. 21, ii. 19), and as a sacrifice of the clan (1 Sam. xx. 6, 29, &c.).

The ancient communion sacrifice, like that described in Leviticus, was a joyous sacrifice, of which the priest and offerer, or the people, ate their share, except for the blood, which was poured out, and the fat, which was burned on the altar. We have few indications concerning the details of the ritual. We know at least that customs varied concerning the portion made over to the priests. We do not know what rules were established for the sanctuary at Shiloh, but the sons of Eli are condemned for not having observed them. They sent their servant to plunge a fork into the cauldron where the meat was cooking, but they demanded one portion of meat raw for roasting, before the fat had been offered to Yahweh (1 Sam. ii. 12–17).[22] In 1 Samuel ix. 23–24, after Samuel had sacrificed, he offered to Saul, his guest, the leg and the tail,[23] although in Leviticus vii. 32 the thigh is the perquisite of the priest, and in Leviticus iii. 9 the tail should be burned before Yahweh. According to Deuteronomy xviii. 3 the priest should receive the shoulder, the cheeks, and the stomach. Finally, as we have seen, Leviticus assigns to him the breast and the right thigh, still raw (Lev. vii. 31–34; x. 14–15).

But the most important evolution affects the parts played respectively by the holocaust and the communion sacrifice in the cult. The holocaust, which was exceptional in ancient times, became the regular sacrifice of the Temple, while the frequency of communion sacrifices diminished. Attempts have been made to explain this evolution by the growing influence of sedentary customs suppressing nomadic ones. Shepherds consider themselves mystically united to the animals of their flock. For them every act of slaughter is a sacrifice. The communion sacrifice

[22] I must correct what I have said in *Ancient Israel: Its Life and Institutions*, pp. 427–8. Verses 13–14 represent a *first* fault of the sons of Eli. Cf. *Les Livres de Samuel*[2] (1961), p. 30, n. *a*.

[23] Reading *wᵉhā'alyāh*, 'and the tail', instead of *wᵉheʿālêhā*, 'and what was upon it', which would be a correction introduced to make the passage conform to the prescription of Lev. iii. 9.

maintains the bond between the animal and the protective deity of the flock. For the sedentary dweller the animal is only a possession, which becomes the subject of a sacrificial offering, and thus the normal sacrifice of the sedentary dweller is the holocaust. With the centralization of the cult and the law of the single sanctuary, the ancient prescription of sacrificial slaughtering becomes impracticable, and Deuteronomy xii. 15, 21 ff., has to authorize the non-sacrificial slaughter of animals.[24] The sociological motives here adduced are somewhat unconvincing, and we shall see that the communion sacrifice, no less than the holocaust, has its roots in the sedentary sphere. The principal reason for this evolution seems in fact to have been the centralization of the cult, and, I would add, the growing frequency of public sacrifices. Individual and family sacrifices became rarer, the act of worship became more independent of the personal intentions of the offerers, and consequently that type of sacrifice became predominant in which the offerer's personal role was reduced to a minimum. One can follow the progress in importance attached to the holocaust. According to 2 Kings xvi. 15, in Ahaz's time the daily service of the Temple comprised only one holocaust in the morning.[25] In the post-exilic Temple a morning and evening holocaust were offered (Exod. xxix. 38–42; Num. xxviii. 2–8). For the Sabbath these holocausts were doubled (Num. xxviii. 9–10). They were increased for the new moon (Num. xxviii. 11–15). Holocausts were offered at all the feasts (Num. xxviii. 16–xxix. 11). Numerous holocausts of bulls, rams, and lambs were prescribed for each of the seven days of the feast of Tabernacles, the number of bulls diminishing steadily from thirteen to seven in the course of the week. The eighth day involved a more simple ritual (Num. xxix. 12–38). In this great ordinance of Numbers xxviii–xxix concerning sacrifices, the communion sacrifice is mentioned only at the end and as a private devotion (Num. xxix. 39).

[24] V. Maag, 'Erwägungen zur deuteronomischen Kultzentralisation', in *V.T.* vi (1956), pp. 10–18, especially pp. 17–18.

[25] Again Ezek. xlvi. 13–15.

III. *The Meaning of the Holocaust and the Communion Sacrifice*

This evolution has affected the meaning of the holocaust and the communion sacrifice. Besides, it must be remembered that sacrifice is a complex act, performed in response to several distinct promptings of the religious conscience. However, the different rites give each form of sacrifice a distinct value. The holocaust is above all an act of homage, expressed by a gift. Thus it becomes the perfect type of sacrifice, of homage rendered to God by the total and unreserved making over of a gift, the *ḳorbān*, i.e. the 'offering' *par excellence* (Lev. i *passim*). In its fully developed stage an expiatory force was ascribed to the blood rite in the holocaust (Lev. i. 4) as in all forms of sacrifice (Lev. xvii. 11). The sacrificial code of Leviticus i–x begins precisely with the ritual of the holocaust.

The communion sacrifice has a different meaning. Its joyful character is often emphasized. In numerous passages of the historical books, and also in the ancient codes of Exodus xxiii and xxxiv, as well as in the prophets, it is simply called *zeḇaḥ*. In the Yahwist and Elohist traditions of the Pentateuch, and frequently in the historical books, and also in Ezekiel, it is called *šᵉlāmîm*. The singular form *šelem* is found only in Amos v. 22. The expression *zeḇaḥ šᵉlāmîm* is consistently used in priestly rituals, rarely elsewhere. It is certain that these terms are broadly equivalent, but their diverse etymology and usage permit one to make certain distinctions.

The term *zeḇaḥ* designates all blood sacrifices which involve a ritual meal, and the name is also applied to the Passover sacrifice (Exod. xii. 27; xxxiv. 25). The terms *šᵉlāmîm* or *zeḇaḥ šᵉlāmîm* designate the type of sacrifice in which one portion is offered to God on the altar, where it is burned, and one portion reverts to the offerer to be eaten; *zeḇaḥ* used alone very often bears this restricted sense, but it is *šᵉlāmîm* which specifically designates the communion sacrifice. From a semantic aspect the word is susceptible of several interpretations. The renderings 'peace offering' or 'salvation offering' are inspired by the Greek version, itself based on the constant force of the root *šlm*.[26] If one takes the derivatives *šillēm* and *šillûm*, meaning 'retribution', as one's starting-point, and if the Ugaritic *šlmm*, meaning 'pledges of peace', is adduced as a parallel, it can be said that this sacrifice is a tribute given to God to establish or re-establish good relations between Himself and His faithful. The *šᵉlāmîm* might then be called a covenant sacrifice. In support of this one might point to the part played by the meal (Gen. xxvi. 30, xxxi. 54; Joshua ix. 14) and by the blood (Exod. xxiv. 8) in the sealing of covenants. However, as far as the blood is concerned, this would be proving too much, for since the blood ritual is the same as in the holocaust, it cannot serve to specify the *šᵉlāmîm*. Furthermore it should be noticed that the sprinkling of the 'blood of the covenant' in Exodus xxiv. 8 is distinct from the blood rite which accompanies the holocausts and communion sacrifices offered on this occasion (Exod. xxiv. 6). The term 'communion sacrifice', which we here retain, takes its origin from the rite which is peculiar to this sacrifice. Once Yahweh has accepted the victim and received His portion on the altar, the offerers eat the remainder in a ritual meal. Paul is referring to the sacrifices of Israel when he says: 'Are those who eat the victims not in communion with the altar?' (1 Cor. x. 18) and, with reference to the sacrifices of heathens, he adds: 'I do not wish you to enter into communion with demons' (1 Cor. x. 20).[27]

Should one go further and interpret the communion sacrifice as a meal taken with God? This theory of a communion with the divinity by the consumption of the same victim has been developed, as far as the Semitic peoples are concerned, by Robertson Smith,[28] and has also been extended to other religions by

[26] Cf. J. Scharbert, '*šlm* im Alten Testament', in *Lex Tua Veritas* (*Festschrift H. Junker*) (1961), pp. 205–29. But it is curious that this study does not contain a word on *šᵉlāmîm*.

[27] Cf. in the Old Testament Exod. xxxiv. 15.

[28] W. Robertson Smith, *The Religion of the Semites* (1889). I am citing the second edition, 1899. Cf. pp. 226–7: 'The leading idea in the animal sacrifices of the Semites . . . was not that of a gift made over to the god, but of an act of communion, in which the god and his worshipper unite by partaking of the flesh and blood of a sacred victim.'

Jevons.[29] It is certain that the Mesopotamian form of sacrifice is strongly alimentary in character. The altar is the god's table, on which are laid, at ordinary meal-times, all the kinds of food which humans take for nourishment.[30] The story of Bel and the Dragon is a satire on this conception. The same is true of Egypt, where the gods were fed three times a day.[31] The Canticle of Moses (Deut. xxxii. 38) speaks of the gods of the Canaanites who 'ate the fat of their sacrifices and drank the wine of their libations'. The Ras Shamra tablets describe the gods as eating and drinking the same food as figures in the ritual of sacrifices.[32]

Often the same explanation has been given for Israelite sacrifice, especially the communion sacrifice.[33] Several arguments are adduced in support of this. The altar is called the 'table of Yahweh', and the sacrificial offerings are called 'Yahweh's food' (Ezek. xliv. 7, 16; Mal. i. 7, 12; Lev. xxi. 6, 8, xxii. 25; Num. xxviii. 2).[34] According to Leviticus xxiv. 5–9 loaves were laid on a table before Yahweh. These were the 'shewbread' or, to translate better, the 'personal loaves' of Yahweh.[35] They were renewed every Sabbath. Yahweh, like the gods of the Canaanites, sniffed up the 'sweet savour' of sacrifices (Lev. i. 9, 13, 17; Ezek. vi. 13, xvi. 19, xx. 28). The cereal offering which accompanied the communion sacrifice as well as the holocaust

[29] R. B. Jevons, *Introduction to the History of Religion* (1902), pp. 144–62.

[30] Cf. E. Dhorme, *Les Religions de Babylonie et d'Assyrie* (Mana I. ii) (1945), pp. 220 ff.; cf. the formula (perhaps somewhat extreme) of G. Furlani, *Il sacrificio nella religione dei Semiti di Babilonia e Assiria* (1932): 'Every sacrifice was a meal of the god and nothing else but a meal.'

[31] Cf. H. Bonnet, *Reallexikon der ägyptischen Religionsgeschichte* (1952), p. 547.

[32] W. Herrmann, 'Götterspeise und Göttertrank in Ugarit und Israel', in *Z.A.W.* lxxii (1960), pp. 205–16.

[33] Cf. in particular A. Wendel, *Das Opfer in der altisraelitischen Religion* (1927), pp. 32–56; W. O. E. Oesterley, *Sacrifices . . .*, pp. 153, 181–7. W. Eichrodt, *Theologie des Alten Testaments I*^{6}, p. 84, holds that sacrifice is originally the offering of food to the divinity, and he finds the influence of this idea in the cultic language and rites of Israel.

[34] Cf. L. Rost, 'Zu den Festopferschriften von Numeri xxviii und xxix', in *T.L.Z.* lxxxiii (1958), cols. 329–34.

[35] Current translations are inaccurate: *leḥem pānîm* is the 'personal bread' of Yahweh, just as *šulḥan pānîm* (Num. iv. 7) is the 'personal table' of Yahweh. Cf. A. R. Johnson, 'Aspects of the Use of the Term *pānîm* in the Old Testament', in *Festschrift O. Eissfeldt* (1947), pp. 155–9.

comprised bread, oil, and wine (Num. xv. 1–12; cf. Exod. xxix. 40; Lev. xxiii. 13), and these constituted the staple diet in ancient Palestine.[36] Salt, the indispensable seasoning for any meal, was added to the cereal offerings (Lev. ii. 13) and to the sacrifices (Ezek. xliii. 24).

These rites and cultic terms occur in recent passages, dating from a period in which it was certainly not believed that Yahweh nourished Himself on the sacrifices offered Him. But it remains a possibility that they are a relic of a more primitive conception. It is a fact that the rite of the shewbread is attested in the time of Saul (1 Sam. xxi. 4–7 (EVV. 4–6)). Bread and wine offerings accompany the sacrifice of Hannah at Shiloh (1 Sam. i. 24) and are carried to Bethel with the animal victim by the pilgrims of 1 Samuel x. 3. The parable of Jotham speaks of oil 'by which gods and men are honoured', and of 'wine which cheers gods and men' (Judges ix. 9, 13). Bread and wine are offered to Yahweh in Hosea ix. 4.

Certain factors must, however, be pointed out. The expressions 'food of Yahweh', 'table of Yahweh', are introduced during the Exile and in a Babylonian environment. They simply bear witness to the Yahwistic religion's power of assimilation: it borrows and adapts to its own use the terms and customs of a foreign cult.[37] The expression 'sweet savour' is used for the first time in connexion with the sacrifices of Noah after the Flood (Gen. viii. 21). In this passage it is an echo, although a weakened one, of the Babylonian Epic of the Flood, with which the biblical account has so many exact parallels. The Babylonian Noah says: 'I offered a sacrifice, I poured out a libation on the top of the mountain. Seven and seven cult-vessels I set up. Upon their plate-stands I heaped cane, cedarwood, and myrtle. The gods smelled the savour, the gods smelled the sweet savour, the gods crowded like flies about the sacrificer.'[38] It will be apparent that

[36] Cf. G. Dalman, *Arbeit und Sitte in Palästina IV*, 'Brot, Öl und Wein' (1935), preface.

[37] Cf. also in Ezekiel the cherubim, the throne of Yahweh, and the description of the altar in the future Temple.

[38] Poem of Gilgamesh, xi. 155–61, in Pritchard, *Ancient Near Eastern*

the borrowed idea has been purged of its grosser elements, and it is noteworthy that in the Babylonian poem itself the 'sweet savour' comes not from the sacrificed meat but from the fragrant woods which are burned on the occasion of the sacrifice. The 'personal loaves' of Yahweh are not carried on to the altar. They are changed every week. Yahweh does not eat them. The parable of Jotham emanates from a Canaanite milieu, and it is noteworthy that Psalms civ. 15, which is inspired by it, suppresses the mention of the gods, and speaks only of wine gladdening the heart of man and oil making faces to shine.

The fact remains that the cereal offering of flour, oil, wine, and salt which accompanied the holocaust and the communion sacrifice does serve to give these sacrifices the appearance of a meal offered to, or shared with, God. The ritual of Numbers xv. 1–12, which determines which offerings are to be made with each type of sacrifice, is probably later than the sacrificial code of Leviticus i–x, but a chapter on cereal offerings was already included in the latter (Lev. ii) and the passages which we have cited prove that the custom was ancient. Yet it is manifest that this custom of offering agricultural produce began only after the settlement of the tribes, and it is highly probable that it was borrowed from the Canaanites.

The isolated and exceptional instances of Gideon's (Judges vi. 18–22) and Manoah's (Judges xiii. 15–20) sacrifices should not be adduced[39] to prove the 'alimentary' character of Israelite sacrifice. These ancient accounts prove rather that the idea of Yahweh being able to feed on sacrifices was rejected. Out of hospitality, Gideon and Manoah wish to offer a meal to the Angel of Yahweh, whom they have not recognized. But in both cases the meal is turned into a holocaust. The Angel of Yahweh says to Manoah: 'Even if you insist, I will not eat of your meal' (Judges xiii. 16). But it is possible, and even probable, that under Canaanite influence, popular religion had interpreted sacrifices

Texts, p. 95. Cf. A. Heidel, *The Gilgamesh Epic and Old Testament Parallels* (1946), pp. 87 and 256.

[39] As Wendel does, op. cit., p. 53.

as meals offered to Yahweh, and Psalms l. 12–13 would be a protest against this deviation:[40]

> If I were hungry, I would not tell you,
> for the world is mine and all that it contains.
> Shall I eat the flesh of bulls?
> Shall I drink the blood of goats?

The reason for the pouring out of the blood and the burning of the fat on the altar is not that Yahweh feeds on them, but that the blood and fat belong to Yahweh alone. The blood contains the life; in fact it is itself the life. That is why man has no right to consume the blood (Gen. ix. 4; Lev. vii. 27, xvii. 14; Deut. xii. 23). That is also why it is given to God. It is quite unnecessary to look for further reasons. The expiatory power attributed to the blood by Leviticus xvii. 11, as also that ascribed to the holocaust on account of the blood rite in Leviticus i. 4, is the result of a later theological development.[41] The offering of fat is to be explained in the same way. 'All fat belongs to Yahweh' (Lev. iii. 16). Hence the fat, like the blood, is forbidden to man (Lev. iii. 17, vii. 23–25). The blood and the fat are carried on to the altar not as food for Yahweh, but as parts belonging exclusively to Yahweh. It is significant that in the communion sacrifice only the blood and the fat are offered to Yahweh, all flesh being excluded. It is not a meal which God shares with His faithful.[42]

IV. *The Origin of the Holocaust and the Communion Sacrifice*

The origin of these sacrificial forms must certainly not be sought in Mesopotamia, where neither holocaust nor communion sacrifice is known. The sacrifice is a meal of the god,

[40] This is not a rejection of an idea which Yahwism had accepted at an earlier stage, as W. Herrmann says, *Z.A.W.* lxxii (1960), p. 214.

[41] Cf. A. Charbel, 'Virtus sanguinis non expiatoria in sacrificiis *šᵉlāmîm*', in *Sacra Pagina* (*Miscellanea Biblica Congressus Internationalis Catholici de Re Biblica*) *I* (1959), pp. 366–76; cf. below, p. 93.

[42] N. H. Snaith, 'Sacrifices in the Old Testament', in *V.T.* vii (1957), pp. 308–17, especially p. 310.

from which the king-priest, the clergy, and the personnel of the temple receive their part. This is determined by certain liturgical texts. It is inaccurate, however, to speak of a communion sacrifice in this connexion,[43] for the offerer receives nothing. It is a levy taken by the cultic functionaries. The blood plays a quite secondary role. It is doubtful, indeed, whether it comes into the rites at all, for blood libations are not attested for normal sacrifices. In the ordinary ritual, nothing is burned on the altar. An animal, or certain parts of an animal, were burned only in certain ceremonies of purification, consecration, or conjuration, and these might also carry with them a smearing with blood. These two rites, which are foreign to the normal Mesopotamian ritual, and which appear only in late texts, are probably borrowed from West Semitic sources.[44]

We have pointed out the close affinities between the sacrifices of the ancient Arabs and the Passover sacrifice,[45] and in this connexion we have remarked on the importance of the blood rite, which is found in other forms of Israelite sacrifice. On the other hand the sacrifice in which the victim is burned on the altar, either wholly or partially, is unknown in central and northern Arabia, apart from some frontier regions.[46] The existence of the holocaust in the regions of southern Arabia is admitted by certain authors,[47] and a cult object called *mṣrb*, formed from a root meaning 'to burn', is interpreted as an altar of holocausts by G. Ryckmans.[48] However, the only inscription in which this cult object is specified speaks of a *mṣrb* of myrrh

[43] As E. Dhorme does, *Les Religions de Babylonie et d'Assyrie*, p. 230.

[44] G. Furlani, *Il sacrificio . . .*, pp. 249–50.

[45] Cf. p. 17.

[46] J. Wellhausen, *Reste arabischen Heidentums*² (1897), pp. 82, 116; W. Robertson Smith, *The Religion of the Semites*, p. 114; J. Henninger, 'Les Fêtes de printemps chez les Arabes et leurs implications historiques', in *Revista do Museu Paulista* (São Paulo) iv (1950), p. 398, n. 23 (with references); G. Klameth, 'Das Opfer bei den Arabern', in *Compte-Rendu de la IIIᵉ semaine d'ethnologie religieuse, 1922* (1923), pp. 312–13.

[47] Cf. the references given by J. Henninger, 'Das Opfer in den altsüdarabischen Hochkulturen', in *Anthropos* xxxvii–xl (1942–5), pp. 779–810, especially pp. 795, 797, 805.

[48] G. Ryckmans, *Les Religions arabes préislamiques*³ (1960), p. 217.

and a *mṣrb* of fragrant wood,[49] and the word may refer always to an altar of perfumes.[50] There is also a verb *hnr*, 'burn', or 'offer a burnt sacrifice', but the context never speaks of an animal victim, and the practice of offering incense provides an adequate explanation of the term. The excavations of the temple of Hureidha in Hadramaut have brought to light altars and great quantities of bones of goats and sheep[51] in the annexes of the sanctuary. But these discoveries do not prove that the altars in question were used for holocausts. They show rather the contrary, for the bones are not burned.[52] Pre-Islamic Arabia, therefore, does not have any equivalent to the holocaust or communion sacrifice.

On the other hand these two forms of sacrifice were certainly known to the Canaanites. According to the Bible, Canaanite sacrifices were distinguished neither by their principal rites nor by their names from Israelite ones. In the scene on Carmel (1 Kings xviii) the holocaust of the prophets of Baal is prepared in the same way as that of Elijah, and the sense of the story requires that this must be the regular form for a sacrifice to Baal. When Jehu offers *z^e^b̲āḥîm* and *'ôlôt̲* in the temple of Baal at Samaria, in the presence of the disciples of Baal, he is certainly following the Canaanite ritual. The Canaanites held sacrificial meals, to which the Israelites were in danger of being invited (Exod. xxxiv. 15 ff.). The same forms of sacrifice are found also among the peoples who settled, about the same time as the Israelites, on the borders of the land of Canaan. Balak, king of Moab, offered holocausts (Num. xxiii). Mesha, another king of Moab, offered his son in holocaust (2 Kings iii. 27). There were Moabites, Ammonites, and Sidonians in Solomon's harem, who offered incense and sacrifice to their gods (1 Kings xi. 8). Naaman the Syrian offered holocausts and communion sacrifices to other gods, but after his miraculous healing he promised

[49] *Répertoire d'épigraphie sémitique*, 2869, 5.

[50] The word is found again in *C.I.S.* iv. 337, 9, and in *Répertoire d'épigraphie sémitique*, 2980 bis, 3 (two *mṣrb*); 3401, 3.

[51] G. Caton-Thompson, *The Tombs and Moon Temple of Hureidha* (*Hadhramaut*) (1944), pp. 45, 46, 48.

[52] Ibid., p. 46.

to offer them only to Yahweh (2 Kings v. 17). It must be concluded, then, that a close similarity existed between Canaanite and Israelite sacrifice, but the Bible does not prove of itself that the technical terms which designated these sacrifices were the same in Canaan and Israel.

We possess no contemporary information of Phoenician provenance by which to check this biblical evidence, but we do have documents coming from the Phoenician colony of Carthage which are later than the biblical texts, and also documents which are earlier than the settlement of the Israelites in the land of Canaan, the Ras Shamra texts.

In the first category, the most important documents are the great sacrificial tariff of Marseilles (so called because the stone was carried thither from North Africa), and the tariff of Carthage.[53] These texts determine the taxes in silver, the portion of the priest, and the portion of the offerer for each type of sacrifice, but they give no description of the rites, or of the motives attached to the various sacrifices. The tariff of Marseilles distinguishes three types of sacrifice: the *kll*, the *ṣwʿt*, and the *šlm kll*. In the *kll* a very small portion of the flesh reverts to the priest and nothing is given to the offerer. In the *ṣwʿt* the breast and thigh go to the priest, the rest is for the offerer. For the *šlm kll* the tariff gives no indication of how the flesh is to be apportioned, except that when a fowl is offered for the purpose of exorcisms or the taking of auspices, the flesh reverts to the offerer. In comparing these sacrifices with the ritual of Leviticus, the *kll* has been identified with the sin offering, the *ṣwʿt* with the communion sacrifice, and the *šlm kll* with the holocaust.[54] These

[53] The tariff of Marseilles is published in *C.I.S.* i. 165. The tariff of Carthage in *C.I.S.* i. 167; to this must be added 3915, 3916, 3917. The most important study is still R. Dussaud's *Les Origines cananéennes du sacrifice israélite*[2] (1941), pp. 134–73 (commentary), 320–3 (translation). Add: S. Langdon, 'The History and Significance of Carthaginian Sacrifice', in *J.B.L.* xxiii (1904), pp. 79–93; D. M. L. Urie, 'Sacrifice among the West Semites', in *P.E.Q.* (1949), pp. 67–82, especially pp. 67–71; J. G. Février, 'Remarques sur le grand tarif dit de Marseille', in *Cahiers de Byrsa* viii (1958–9), pp. 35–43.

[54] Thus Dussaud, Février. But H. L. Ginsberg, 'A Punic Note', in *A.J.S.L.* xlvii (1930–1), pp. 52–53, identifies *kll* with the holocaust, *šlm kll* with the

equivalences are uncertain.[55] The clearest is that of the *ṣwʿt* to the communion sacrifice. It should be noticed, however, that the term does not occur in Hebrew and that, in the hypothesis, the other terms designate different sacrifices in the Punic from those which they designate in the Hebrew. The question is still further complicated if one compares the tariff of Carthage, which gives slightly different provisions for the *kll* and the *ṣwʿt*, and which says nothing of the *šlm kll.* To increase the difficulty, *šlm* alone is found in an inscription of Citium,[56] *ʿlt* and *mnḥt* (*ʿôlāh* and *minḥāh* in Hebrew) are found together in a neo-Punic inscription of the Roman epoch.[57]

The texts which have come down to us do not, therefore, permit us to reconstruct a uniform system of Punic sacrifice; still less do they permit us to imagine what Phoenician sacrifice was during the biblical epoch. However, the biblical evidence, coupled with the inscriptions from North Africa, does authorize us to conclude that the Phoenicians, like the Israelites, made use of the holocaust and the communion sacrifice; at the same time it must be recognized that the two systems evolved independently, with different terminologies.

The discoveries of Ras Shamra, ancient Ugarit, have provided a documentation of the fourteenth century B.C., at a period, that is, prior to the settlement of the Israelites in Palestine. The information on sacrifices afforded by these texts has several times been studied and related to the Bible.[58] Turning our attention to vocabulary, and to the points which concern us here, we may

šᵉlāmîm, and *ṣwʿt* with the expiatory sacrifices. This does not take account of the ritual directions given by the tariffs.

[55] Cf. Urie, loc. cit., pp. 69–70.

[56] *C.I.S.* i. 86, B, l. 4.

[57] Inscription of Althiburos l. 8, G. A. Cooke, *North-Semitic Inscriptions*, No. 55, cf. J. G. Février, in *R.H.R.* cxliii (1953—A), p. 17.

[58] Th. H. Gaster, 'The Service of the Sanctuary: A Study in Hebrew Survivals', in *Mélanges Syriens offerts à R. Dussaud II* (1939), pp. 577–82; R. Dussaud, *Les Origines cananéennes du sacrifice israélite*² (1941), pp. 326 ff.; D. M. L. Urie, *Sacrifice among the West Semites*, in *P.E.Q.* (1949), pp. 67–82, especially pp. 71–80; J. Gray, 'Cultic Affinities between Israel and Ras Shamra', in *Z.A.W.* lxii (1950), pp. 207–20; A. De Guglielmo, 'Sacrifice in the Ugaritic Texts', in *C.B.Q.* xvii (1955), pp. 196–216; J. Gray, *The Legacy of Canaan* (Supplement to *V.T.* v) (1957), pp. 140–52.

notice that *dbḥ*, 'sacrifice', corresponds to *zeḇaḥ*. The words *šlm* or *šlmm* correspond to *šᵉlāmîm*; the terms appear several times in the minor rituals,[59] and what is possibly a divinized form of *šlm* occurs in a list of the gods of Ugarit which has been preserved in alphabetic writing,[60] and in Akkadian transcription, where the word is rendered as *salimu*.[61] The term *'ôlāh* is absent from the Ras Shamra texts, but the word *šrp*, 'burnt offering', which is associated with *šlmm* in two cultic texts,[62] may be equivalent to it and may designate the holocaust. Unfortunately these brief references do not give any indication of the rites which were followed. More revealing, perhaps, are the descriptions of certain cultic acts in the poems of Ras Shamra. The sacrifice offered by the hero, Keret, is especially interesting:

> He washed, yea, rouged himself (i.e. 'painted himself' rather than 'rubbed himself with blood'); he washed his hands to the elbow, from his fingers to the shoulder. He entered into the shade of a tent. He took a lamb of sacrifice in his hand, a young beast in both hands, all his best food; he took . . . (?) a bird of sacrifice, he poured wine into a cup of silver, honey into a cup of gold; and he went up to the top of the tower, he mounted on the shoulder of the wall; he lifted up his hands to heaven, and he sacrificed to the Bull El, his father, he honoured Baal with his sacrifice, the son of Dagan with his offering.[63]

The cereal offering and the mention of wine in addition to the animal victim should be noted. There is a correspondence in this respect with the Israelite *minḥāh*. Then Keret redescends and prepares food for the city, but this new action bears no apparent relationship to the sacrifice, so that this would be a holocaust.[64] An allusion to the communion sacrifice can be discerned in the Legend of Aqhat, in connexion with the duties of Danel's son, 'who eats his meal in the temple of Baal, his portion in the temple of El'.[65]

[59] Gordon, **1.** 4; **3.** 17, 52; **5.** 7; **9.** 7, 15.
[60] Gordon, **17.** 12.
[61] Cf. J. Nougayrol, *C.R.A.I.* (1957), p. 83; E. Weidner, *A.f.O.* xviii (1957), p. 170.
[62] Gordon, **1.** 4; **9.** 7.
[63] Gordon, *Krt*, 156–71.
[64] But this sacrifice is called *dbḥ* in the text.
[65] Gordon, 2 *Aqht*, i. 32–33.

The holocaust, the communion sacrifice, and the cereal offering accompanying them can thus be rediscovered at Ras Shamra and later in Phoenicia and North Africa. There is, however, one rite which is essential to Israelite sacrifice, yet which is absent here; it is the blood rite. It is true that attempts have been made to discern this in the passage of Keret which we have cited; the beginning of this is rendered: 'He rubbed himself with blood.'[66] The accuracy of this translation is extremely doubtful; even if it were accurate, it would signify, rather, an act of consecration on the part of the offerer, preparatory to the sacrifice itself.[67] The most important element of the Israelite sacrifice would still be lacking: the contact of the victim's blood with the altar.

The holocaust and communion sacrifice, then, accompanied by a cereal offering, are common to the Canaanites and Israelites alike; they were also practised, according to the biblical evidence, among the Moabites and Aramaeans of Damascus, but they were unknown in Mesopotamia and Arabia. Now it is striking that these two sacrifices, which are proper to the West Semites, should also be Greek sacrifices.[68] In Greece the holocaust, although rare, is not unknown (just as the *'ôlāh* was at first far rarer than the *šᵉlāmîm*). It was offered in honour of the chthonic gods, the heroes, and the dead; the victim was usually burned not on the ordinary altar of sacrifices, but on a special altar which was improvised, and which was burned with the victim.[69] Far the most frequent sacrifice was the θυσία; moreover, it is almost always by this word that the Septuagint trans-

[66] Cf. R. Dussaud, *Les Origines cananéennes . . .*, pp. 328–30.

[67] J. Gray, *Z.A.W.* lxii (1950), p. 217, compares the anointing of Aaron and his sons with the blood of the ram sacrificed for their investiture, Exod. xxix. 19–21; Lev. viii. 22–24.

[68] The correspondences have been established by R. K. Yerkes, *Sacrifice in Greek and Roman Religions and Early Judaism* (1952). These correspondences have been made use of by L. Rost, 'Erwägungen zum israelitischen Brandopfer', in *Von Ugarit nach Qumran: Festschrift O. Eissfeldt* (Beihefte zur *Z.A.W.* 77) (1958), pp. 177–83.

[69] M. P. Nilsson, *Geschichte der griechischen Religion I* (1941), p. 121. Cf. S. Eitrem, 'Opferritus und Voropfer der Griechen und Römer', in *Kristiana Videnskapsselskaps Skriften, II Hist. filol. Klasse* (1914), No. 1.

lates *zeḇaḥ*. After the victim was slaughtered and cut in pieces, the thighs and other pieces of meat, the fat, and the bones were placed on the altar and burned, while libations of wine were poured out on the offerings. The remainder was eaten by the faithful. As a sacrifice, therefore, the *θυσία* is very similar to the Israelite communion sacrifice, but no blood rite is provided for; the blood is simply allowed to flow down into the ground. The custom of anointing the altar with blood is secondary; it derives from the sacrifices offered to the dead and to the chthonic gods.[70]

This close similarity between sacrifices practised by the Greeks and the West Semites, in contrast to the rest of the Semitic sphere, can only be explained by supposing either that one derives from the other, or that both derive from a common origin. One might conceivably accord some priority to Greece, and attempt to explain the introduction of these rites into Canaan by the influence of the Mycenaeans, who had markets on the coast of Asia. Just such a market is known to have existed at Ras Shamra, whence our earliest witnesses derive. It is doubtful, however, whether these commercial relations could have affected religious customs so deeply, and the hypothesis of a common origin seems preferable. In that case these rites would be the relics of a civilization spread throughout the eastern Mediterranean basin before the installation of the Hellenes and the Canaanites. In fact other contacts can be pointed to in the cult and its vocabulary: *βωμός* meaning both 'dais' and 'altar' and *bāmāh* the 'high place' which served as an altar; *μάζα* 'barley bread' and *maṣṣāh* 'unleavened bread'; *μῶμος* 'blame' and *m*[e]*'ûm* 'fault'. The wine, which had a part to play in Greek, Canaanite, and Israelite sacrifices, has a name which is common to the two groups: *yayn*, *οἶνος*. It should be noted that these words cannot be explained—or at least not without difficulty—by either a Semitic or a Greek root.

[70] M. P. Nilsson, op. cit., p. 139; J. H. Waszink, *Reallexikon für Antike und Christentum II* (1954), s.v. 'Blut', cols. 460–1.

The hypothesis can be proposed, therefore, that the Canaanites borrowed the holocaust and communion sacrifice from a pre-Semitic civilization, and the Ras Shamra texts indicate that they were in possession of these cultic forms before the Israelites were settled in Palestine. The latter, in their semi-nomadic period, would have known only one form of sacrifice, the Passover type, the *zeḇaḥ*, the closest analogies to which are to be found in ancient Arabian sacrifices.[71] When they gained possession of the Holy Land, the Israelites would have borrowed the holocaust and the communion sacrifice from the Canaanites, together with the cereal offerings which accompanied them. According to the Ras Shamra texts the communion sacrifice was then called *šlmm*,[72] and the name would have been borrowed at the same time as the rite. The pseudo-plural form *šᵉlāmîm* is explicable on these grounds, and it can be compared to other loan-words in the religious vocabulary: *'ûrîm*, *tummîm*, *tᵉrāp̄îm*, which, in their primitive form, are singulars with mimation.[73] On the same grounds one might justify the use of the term *zᵉḇāḥîm šᵉlāmîm* in Exodus xxiv. 5; 1 Samuel xi. 15; cf. Joshua xxii. 27. These two words are in apposition, and one must be an explanatory gloss upon the other. Finally this hypothesis would explain why *zeḇaḥ*, the term for the primitive sacrifice in which the victim was sacrificed and eaten, should also have been kept for the communion sacrifice, in which part of the sacrificed victim was eaten by the believers.

However, this is no servile borrowing, and the Israelite sacrifices preserved their originality. The character of a meal shared with the divinity which was common to the Canaanite communion sacrifice and the Greek θυσία was obscured by the choice of portions offered to Yahweh in the Israelite *šᵉlāmîm*: none of the lean meat was burned on the altar. Above all the

[71] Cf. p. 17 and the discussion of references to the holocaust and communion sacrifice before the settlement.

[72] Let us recall that the singular form *šelem* is found only once, Amos v. 22.

[73] Cf. A. Jirku, 'Die Mimation in den nordsemitischen Sprachen und einige Bezeichnungen der altisraelitischen Mantik', in *Biblica* xxxiv (1953), pp. 78–80.

blood rites, which found no part either in Canaanite or Greek sacrifice, became an essential element in the *'ôlāh* and the *š^e^lāmîm*, and thus ensured the basic continuity between these new forms, and the ancient *zeḇaḥ* form of sacrifice, which was perpetuated in the Passover.

III

HUMAN SACRIFICES IN ISRAEL

IN the general history of religions it has often been admitted that animal victims were substitutes for human victims and that human sacrifices came before animal sacrifices. This theory can no longer be defended. If we abide by what really constitutes a sacrifice, i.e. the putting to death of a human being not merely in the course of any sort of religious action, not merely in a holy place, but specifically as a victim offered to the divinity, then human sacrifice hardly appears in religions styled 'primitive'. On the contrary, the practice only develops among peoples who have attained a certain level of culture.[1] This general conclusion holds good for the Semitic milieu to which we confine ourselves: human sacrifice is attested most clearly in some societies which are relatively evolved and prosperous materially while morally decadent, as were Phoenicia and Carthage.[2] We shall first investigate the practice of Israel's neighbours, then we shall inquire whether human sacrifices were offered by Israelites, and whether they were ever looked upon as lawful. Finally we shall study the particular problem of sacrifices to Moloch.

I. *Human Sacrifices outside Israel*

I. *Pre-islamic Arabia*[3]

First let us set aside a text which historians of religion have used

[1] E. Westermarck, *Origin and Development of the Moral Ideas* (1906–8), i. 436: 'The practice of human sacrifices cannot be regarded as characteristic of savage races. On the contrary it is found much more frequently among barbarians and semi-civilised peoples than among genuine savages, and at the lowest stages of culture known to us it is hardly heard of.'

[2] J. Henninger, 'Über Menschenopfer bei den vorislamischen Arabern', in *Akten des vierundzwanzigsten internationalen Orientalisten-Kongresses 1957* (1959), pp. 244–6.

[*for footnote 3 see p. 53*

all too readily: it is that autobiographical narrative attributed to St. Nilus, who is said to have been a hermit at Sinai in the fourth–fifth centuries of our era.[4] He tells how his son was made a prisoner by the Saracens, who decided to offer him as a holocaust to the Morning Star (the goddess al-ʿUzza) as was their wont to do with any fine young men whom they made captive. All was ready, altar, wood, and sword; but the barbarians woke up too late: the planet whose presence was necessary had disappeared, and the young man was saved. The author then explains that, failing human victims, the Saracens would sacrifice a camel, which they would devour before sunrise, uncooked, and without leaving a scrap. It is upon this text that Robertson Smith based his theory of Semitic sacrifice.[5] But all this narrative is fiction without historical basis,[6] and its description of sacrifice is contradicted by almost all we know from elsewhere about the rites of Arabs.[7]

There is only one single epigraphic text as evidence for human sacrifice in Arabia, and its interpretation is doubtful. In a Liḥyanite inscription, previous to our era, three personages consecrate to their god a slave in their possession, and the first editors explain that he has been sacrificed.[8] This interpretation is not absolutely excluded, but it is much more probable that we have here simply the dedication of a slave to temple service.[9] The only attestations we can retain are of a literary character. I take them in chronological order. According to Porphyry in the third century, the inhabitants of Duma sacrificed a child each

[3] Cf. especially J. Henninger, 'Menschenopfer bei den Arabern', in *Anthropos* liii (1958), pp. 721–805. The conclusions of this article are summed up in the communication cited in the preceding note.

[4] Migne, *P.G.* lxxix, cols. 583–694.

[5] *The Religion of the Semites*, 2nd ed. (1894), *passim*. Cf. M.-J. Lagrange, *Études sur les religions sémitiques*² (1905), pp. 257–9.

[6] Cf. R. Devreesse in *Vivre et Penser I* (= *R.B.* xlix) (1940), pp. 220–2.

[7] J. Henninger, 'Ist der sogenannte Nilus-Bericht eine brauchbare religionsgeschichtliche Quelle?', in *Anthropos* l (1955), pp. 81–148.

[8] A. Jaussen and R. Savignac, *Mission archéologique en Arabie II* (1914), No. 49. Cf. pp. 381–2.

[9] W. Caskel, *Lihyan und Lihyanisch* (1954), p. 48; J. Henninger, 'Menschenopfer . . .', p. 745 and n. 73.

year and buried it under the altar.[10] According to Isaac of Antioch, in the fifth century, the Arabs of the Syrian desert, after having captured Beth-Ḥur on the Euphrates, sacrificed numerous boys and girls to Kaukabta (who is al-ʿUzza).[11] In the sixth century, the Lakhmid Mundhir III captured Emesus, and, it is said, offered to this same goddess four hundred nuns. And when in the course of a *razzia* he went off with the son of his enemy the Ghassanid Harith, he sacrificed him too to al-ʿUzza.[12] There were near Kufa two stelae called Gharîyâni, 'the two stelae rubbed with blood'. The legend has it that they were set up by Mundhir, who used to anoint them every year with the blood of human victims.[13] At Mecca an age-old tradition had it that Mahomet's grandfather vowed that he would sacrifice one of his sons when the tenth should be born; after the birth, lots were drawn for the victim, and Mahomet's father was designated, but he was redeemed by an offering of one hundred camels. Again at Mecca, in the early days of Islam, a woman had vowed to sacrifice her expected son; she was advised to offer a hundred camels in his stead. The governor of Medina, however, simply declared the vow invalid.[14]

No trace can be found of human sacrifice in the whole of southern Arabia. For northern Arabia we have cited all the examples worthy of note: they are sparse and late in their attestations. They are found in frontier regions (the Lakhmids of Ḥira, the Arabs of the Syrian desert) and at halting-points of trade routes (Duma, Mecca). Further we should note that for

[10] Porphyry, *De Abstinentia*, ii. 56; reproduced by Eusebius, *Praep. Ev.* (ed. Maas), iv. 16, 8.

[11] Quoted by J. Wellhausen, *Reste arabischen Heidentums*² (1897), p. 40.

[12] Procopius of Gaza, *De Bello Persico*, ii. 28, 13; Zacariah the Rhetor (J. P. N. Land, *Anecdota Syriaca* iii, p. 247; trans. F. J. Hamilton and E. W. Brooks, pp. 206–7); Michael the Syrian, ix. 16 (trans. Chabot, ii, pp. 178–9). Cf. Wellhausen, *Reste* . . ., pp. 43 and 115; R. Devreesse, *Vivre et Penser II* (= *R.B.* li) (1942), pp. 281 and 294; R. Aigrain, art. 'Arabie', in the *Dictionnaire d'histoire et de géographie ecclésiastiques*, col. 1227.

[13] The tradition has different forms, cf. Wellhausen, *Reste* . . ., p. 43; G. Rothstein, *Die Dynastie der Laḫmiden im El-Ḥîra* (1899), pp. 141–2; R. Aigrain, art. 'Arabie', col. 1229.

[14] Wellhausen, *Reste* . . ., p. 116; J. Chelhod, *Le Sacrifice chez les Arabes* (1955), pp. 97–98; M. Gaudefroy-Demombynes, *Mahomet* (1957), p. 57.

Mundhir and the Arabs of the Syrian desert (in the story of Pseudo-Nilus) prisoners of war are involved. In the two cases at Mecca we can only conclude that the idea of human sacrifice was not unknown at the outset of Islam, but that its practice was condemned. We shall see that among the Canaanites, where human sacrifice is best attested, it is in relation to a fertility cult. Thus it would seem that it was practised first in agricultural civilizations and only subsequently at a late period penetrated into Arabia, where it is confined to those regions and centres which had greater contact with the exterior.[15]

2. *Mesopotamia*

L. Woolley discovered at Ur sixteen 'royal' tombs in which the dead person had been buried together with a sometimes quite large retinue of guards, servants, and women. Some have held that we have here a rite in which those who participated first mimed the sacred marriage of the god and then were sacrificed to promote fertility.[16] This hypothesis was effectively refuted by Woolley, who takes them to be human sacrifices offered to the defunct king now deified.[17] A counter argument is that one of the tombs is that of queen Shubad, who was certainly not deified. Nor is it proved that the other tombs are those of kings. The most plausible explanation is that the departed one kept—or was given—for his service beyond the grave the personnel which he had during life.[18]

[15] These are the conclusions of Henninger, which coincide with those already expressed by Th. Nöldeke in Hastings, *Encyclopædia of Religion and Ethics I*, 665*b*; cf. also M. Guidi, *Storia e Cultura degli Arabi fino alla morte di Maometto* (1951), p. 138.

[16] S. Smith, *Journal of the Royal Asiatic Society* (1928), pp. 849–68; F. de Liagre Böhl, 'Das Menschenopfer bei den alten Sumerer', in *Z.A.* xxxix (1929), pp. 83–98, reproduced in his *Opera Minora* (1953), pp. 163–73.

[17] L. Woolley, *Ur Excavations. II. The Royal Cemetery* (1934), pp. 33–42.

[18] N. Schneider, 'Die Religion der Sumerer', in Fr. König (ed.), *Christ und die Religionen der Erde II* (1952), pp. 434–5. Woolley himself recognizes that the term 'sacrifice' is incorrect and ends, op. cit., pp. 41–42, by suggesting an explanation which is very close to the one we have adopted. We can compare two texts of the Assyrian period difficult to interpret: a 'king substitute' (cf. below) is accompanied in death by his 'lady of the palace' (Harper, *Assyrian*

Besides there is no sure proof that human sacrifice was ever practised in Mesopotamia. Yet an attempt has been made to suggest an example in history. Ashurbanipal says that he has struck down the murderers of his grandfather 'as his funeral sacrifice'.[19] Though not all would agree,[20] still I maintain that the expression should be taken in a figurative sense: the punishment of the murderers, executed in the very place where they have committed their crime, is compared to a funeral offering presented to the departed person.[21]

Some have also argued from what is incorrectly termed 'substitution sacrifices'. Sickness was held to result from the vengeance of the gods or the wickedness of demons. To divert these, an animal was taken and treated as *puḫu* or vicar or *dinânu*, the substitute of the sick person. This animal was slain by the exorcizer-priest to the accompaniment of magical formulae. Here is a specimen:

> A lamb is a substitute for man
> he has given the lamb for his life,
> he has given head of lamb for head of man
> he has given neck of lamb for neck of man
> he has given breast of lamb for breast of man.[22]

The animal is handed over as a prey to the devil who is to be diverted from the man. It is a magical action and not a sacrifice.[23] Least of all can it be a dim relic of a human sacrifice wherein the

and Babylonian Letters, No. 437); according to a ritual for a king's funeral, the 'fiancée' or 'lady of the palace' is walled up in the tomb (E. Ebeling, *Tod und Leben nach den Vorstellungen der Babylonier I* (1931), No. 14; cf. W. von Soden, *Z.A.* xlv (1939), pp. 42–61; E. Dhorme, *R.A.* xxxviii (1941), pp. 57–66. But we cannot follow H. Frankfort, who explains the tombs of Ur as those of 'king substitutes' put to death with their suite, *Kingship and the Gods* (1948), pp. 264 and 400, n. 12.

[19] Rassam cylinder, iv. 70–73.

[20] In particular, E. Dhorme, *R.H.R.* cvii (1933), i, p. 115.

[21] Cf. G. Furlani, *Il sacrificio della religione dei Semiti di Babilonia e Assiria* (1932), pp. 147–9. All the more so as the term employed, *kispu*, denotes properly speaking a food offering to the dead.

[22] The series *Utukki limnûti*, *C.T.* xvii, pl. vi. iii. 15.

[23] Thus Furlani, op. cit., pp. 113–14; against E. Dhorme, loc. cit., pp. 110–11.

animal victim was substituted for a human victim, because the animal is a substitute for *the offerer*.[24]

Nor can we any the more see a sacrifice, still less the equivalent of a human sacrifice, in a rite which is referred to in certain vassalage treaties. In the treaty which Ashurnirari VI of Assyria imposed on Mati'ilu of Arpad,[25] a ram is brought and cut up: 'this head is not the head of the ram, it is the head of Mati'ilu, of his sons, of his great ones, of the people of his country. If the aforenamed sin against this treaty, as the head of the ram is cloven . . . so may the head of the aforenamed be cloven; this thigh is not the ram's thigh, it is that of the aforenamed . . .' &c. It is not a sacrifice,[26] and the text says explicitly a few lines above: 'This ram is not brought for sacrifice . . . it is brought for the conclusion of a treaty.' It is a magic action calculated to forestall the breaking of the treaty.[27] This interpretation becomes manifest if we compare the treaty which Bar-Ga'aya of KTK imposed on this same Mati'ilu. Of this three fragmentary Aramaic recensions have been found.[28] According to one of these, a wax figurine—'it is Mati'ilu'—is burnt: 'may Mati'ilu burn thus'; then a calf is cut up, 'may Mati'ilu be thus cut up'.[29]

In the royal correspondence of Assyria, several letters, all dating seemingly from the reign of Esarhaddon, refer to a 'royal substitute' or a 'substitute king' who would assume for a short period the place, attributes, and powers of the real king.[30] By combining these texts with the Babylonian and Persian feast

[24] The case of Punic sacrifices, which we shall study below, is quite different: the lamb is substituted for a human victim.

[25] E. Weidner, *A.f.O.* viii (1932–4), pp. 17–26.

[26] Against E. Dhorme, loc. cit., pp. 112–13.

[27] Thus G. Furlani, op. cit., pp. 181–2.

[28] A. Dupont-Sommer and J. Starcky, 'Une Inscription araméenne inédite de Sfiré (Stèle III)', in *Bulletin du Musée de Beyrouth* xiii (1956), pp. 23–41; id., 'Les Inscriptions araméennes de Sfiré (Stèles I et II)', in *Mémoires présentés par divers savants à l'Académie des Inscriptions et Belles-Lettres* xv (1958), pp. 197–351.

[29] Stele I, A 1°1°. 36–40.

[30] Cf. especially R. Labat, 'Le Sort des substituts royaux en Assyrie', in *R.A.* xl (1945–6), pp. 123–42; R. Gossens, 'Les Substituts royaux en Babylonie', in *Ephemerides Theologicae Lovanienses* xxv (1949), pp. 383–400, where one can find the antecedent bibliography.

of the *Sacaea*, and with Frazer's theory about the magic character of the king and of the cult of the dying god, Ebeling had explained that each year, at the feast of the New Year, the king was given a substitute who was put to death to bring about a renewal of life for the king and prosperity for the country.[31] This hypothesis has been refuted by a better understanding of these texts,[32] and by the publication of a ritual, unfortunately very fragmentary, which relates to the king-substitute.[33] It is now certain that it was not annual and that it had nothing to do with fertility rites: when particularly unpropitious omens obtained, in an eclipse of the moon or of the sun, a substitute would ostensibly exercise the royal power so as to draw away from the king and bring upon himself the danger prognosticated by the omens; once the critical time was over, the king resumed his functions. We are left uncertain about the fate of the substitute at the end of his fictive rule. It is generally held that he was put to death. Admittedly only one single letter speaks of the death of the royal substitute and does so in terms which could suggest, and would better suggest, a natural death by sickness or accident. Nevertheless the ritual recently published says 'the man who has been provided as substitute for the king will die . . . and the evil omens will not affect the king'[34]—which might imply that the substitute had been executed. But the text says 'will die' and not 'will be put to death'. So it is possible that it does not express a ritual action which must be carried out (the prescribed actions in the text are expressed in the second person), but an outcome or the result which was expected of the ritual. This would tally with the letters concerning the royal substitute, where we often find the expression 'let him go to his destiny'. The menace which weighed heavily upon the king has been transferred to his substitute: if the latter died of sickness or by

[31] E. Ebeling, *Tod und Leben* . . ., pp. 62–63.

[32] The last work is that of W. von Soden, 'Beiträge zum Verständnis der neuassyrischen Briefe über die Ersatzkönigsriten', in *Festschrift* . . . *Christian* (1956), pp. 100–7.

[33] W. G. Lambert, 'A Part of the Ritual for the Substitute King', in *A.f.O.* xviii (1957), pp. 109–12.

[34] Lambert, loc. cit., col. A 6–7.

accident, the king was saved; if the substitute did not die during the period when the omens were menacing (a period which could last up to a hundred days, according to one of the letters), the danger incurred by the king was also diverted, and there is no reason left for wishing or procuring the death of the substitute. This interpretation seems to square with all the texts which we have; but even were it proved that the royal substitute was executed, we should not term this magical action a human sacrifice.

Finally, certain Assyrian contracts of the seventh century B.C. contain a curious penal clause. Over and above a fine in silver and gold, he who violates the contract 'will burn his eldest son in the sacred precinct of Adad',[35] or 'will burn for Bêlit-Sêri either his eldest son or his eldest daughter with an *imer* of good spices',[36] or again 'will burn his eldest son for Sin, will burn his eldest daughter for Bêlit-Sêri with a *pa-nu* of cedar'.[37] It has been suggested that *šarâpu* 'burn' here has a weakened sense and would refer to a dedication effected by a fire ritual;[38] it has also been argued that the clause was never applied because its severity prevented the violation of the contract;[39] others recognize here human sacrifices in which the victim was burned, and compare them with the Moloch sacrifices which we shall study below.[40] This last explanation is the most convincing, and we shall recall that these contracts date precisely from the time when sacrifices of children by fire came from Phoenicia and were introduced into Israel, and when this exceptional usage in Mesopotamia resulted from the same influence. This explanation probably also accounts for two inscriptions in the palace of Kapara (tenth century) at Tell Ḥalâf in Upper Mesopotamia: should anyone efface

[35] *T.C.L.* ix. 37, translated in J. Kohler and A. Ungnad, *Assyrische Rechtsurkunden*, No. 41. Cf. C. H. W. Johns, *Assyrian Deeds and Documents*, No. 632 = Kohler–Ungnad No. 160.

[36] Johns No. 310 = Kohler–Ungnad No. 158.

[37] Johns No. 436 = Kohler–Ungnad No. 163; cf. Johns No. 474 = Kohler–Ungnad No. 96*a*.

[38] Johns, op. cit. *III*, pp. 345–6.

[39] G. Furlani, op. cit., p. 171.

[40] Thus Kohler and Ungnad, op. cit., p. 456; E. Dhorme, *R.H.R.* cvii (1933—A), pp. 117–19.

the royal name, seven of his sons are to be burnt before Adad.[41]

3. *Phoenicia*

It is in fact in Phoenicia and in the Canaanite milieu generally that we have the clearest attestations.

First, however, we need to set aside certain evidences which have been wrongly adduced. Palestinian archaeologists of the last generation often spoke of 'sacrifices of children' buried in jars with a few funerary offerings, or of 'foundation sacrifices' whether of children or adults buried against or under the walls of a house or edifice.[42] As a general rule, and perhaps a universal rule, burial of new-born infants under the ground level of houses or grouped in a free space corresponds to the current practice of burying near hearth and home children who die at an early age. As for children or adults buried under or against the base of a building, we should first of all establish that the inhumation was contemporary with the building, and neither anterior nor posterior thereto. Stratigraphic indications in excavators' reports are not always sufficient to settle the matter. Still, in the great majority of cases, one can conclude that the burial was not made for the foundation of the edifice. A few cases, however, are open to debate. At Tell el-Fârʿah near Nablus we have found against the gate of Middle Bronze Age, and lower than its foundations, a jar containing the skeleton of a new-born child, and alongside this jar the burial-place of another new-born child in a niche cut into the base of the masonry of the gate; my hypothesis was that these children had been the victims of a foundation sacrifice.[43] This remains very doubtful; the first tomb seems rather to be related to the Middle Bronze level which precedes the building of the gate, while the second may

[41] B. Meissner, 'Die Keilschrifttexte aus dem Tell Ḥalâf', in *Festschrift M. von Oppenheim* (1933), texts ii and iii, pp. 72–75.

[42] In particular, L. H. Vincent, *Canaan d'après l'exploration récente* (1907), pp. 188–200. Archaeologists are much more cautious nowadays, but the old opinion persists amongst certain biblical scholars, thus in W. Eichrodt, *Theologie des Alten Testaments I*^{6} (1959), p. 88.

[43] These are the tombs J and K, *R.B.* lviii (1951), pp. 401–3.

have been put together by taking away a few stones from the gate which was already built.

For Palestine there remains one literary attestation. When, in the reign of Ahab, Hiel of Bethel rebuilt Jericho, 'at the price of his first-born Abiram he established its foundation, and at the price of his last-born Segub he set up its gates'.[44] We may have here a foundation sacrifice, and the text has often been interpreted in this sense. Yet it may simply mean that during the rebuilding of Jericho Hiel lost two of his sons, and this came to be explained as the fulfilment of an age-old curse pronounced by Joshua.[45] If they are really and truly foundation sacrifices, Phoenician influence, which prevailed in Ahab's time, could account for it.

The Ras Shamra poems include a scene which has a sure relationship to a fertility cult. In order to restore Baal to life and to procure a return to rain and plenty the goddess Anat lays hold of the god Môt, cuts him up with a sword as one cuts sheaves, winnows him as corn is winnowed, roasts him in the fire, crushes him in the mill, and scatters his fragments in the fields, where the birds come to eat them just as they peck at the grain which has been sown.[46] This might be a mythic explanation of the annual renewal of vegetation, but it could also be the mythological transposition of a ritual action which was recurrent in worship: a human sacrifice to assure fertility.

That this is so seems to be proved by the story of Saul's descendants who were executed by the Gibeonites (2 Sam. xxi. 1–14).[47] This execution is a religious action related to fertility;

[44] 1 Kings xvi. 34.

[45] Joshua vi. 26. So, too, most recently, O. Eissfeldt, art. 'Menschenopfer', in *Religion in Geschichte und Gegenwart*[3] (1960), col. 868. The literary relationships of the two biblical passages is moreover complex. Cf. M. Noth, *Palästinajahrbuch*, xxxi (1935), p. 27; id., *Das Buch Josua*[2] (1953), p. 41.

[46] I, AB, ii. 30–37 = Gordon No. 49. The translation of the last three lines is disputed, but it is certainly something to do with birds who eat or do not eat the flesh and the remains of Môt.

[47] The link was established by H. Cazelles, 'David's Monarchy and the Gibeonite Claim', in *P.E.Q.* (1955), pp. 165–75. Already R. Dussaud had hinted at it without going further, *R.H.R.* civ (1931—B), p. 392; A. S. Kapelrud, 'King and Fertility. A Discussion of II Sam. 21. 1–14', in *Interpretationes ad*

it takes place 'before Yahweh', verse 6, it follows upon a long drought which has caused a famine, verse 1, it takes place at harvest time, verse 9, it brings rain, verse 10, cf. verse 14. According to the text, it is to expiate the blood of the Gibeonites shed by Saul and a manner of averting the curse which weighs upon Israel. But the important thing for us is the manner in which these Gibeonites exercise this blood-vengeance: the victims are 'dismembered' or 'dislocated'[48] before Yahweh, their bodies—or their members?—remain exposed, and Rizpah wards off the birds of the sky that would swoop on them: here we find the principal elements of the Ras Shamra text. The Gibeonites are not Israelites, they are descendants of the old population of Canaan: with David's consent, they indulged in a Canaanite fertility rite.

The clearest attestations in the Phoenician world have reference to child sacrifices. We shall have much to say about these when treating of sacrifices which were offered in Israel in imitation of them.

I add one point, not concerning the Canaanites themselves, but still Israel's immediate neighbours, the Moabites. King Mesha, when besieged in his capital by the Israelites, offered his son as a holocaust on the rampart (2 Kings iii. 27). The text stresses the exceptional character of such a sacrifice: the Israelites, terrified by this spectacle, fled straightway.[49]

Vetus Testamentum pertinentes (*Festschrift Mowinckel*) (1955), pp. 113–22; cf. id., 'King David and the Sons of Saul', in *The Social Kingship* (*Congress at Rome*), Supplement IV of *Numen* (1959), pp. 294–301. Kapelrud recognized the ritual character of the execution, but he has not seen the connexion with the text of Ras Shamra. His interpretation oversteps the mark. He explains that to put a stop to the famine, some royal blood must be spilled; there could be no question of David himself, but there was Saul's family, which was handed over probably on some made-up pretext. David accommodated himself to the ideas of his Canaanite subjects and, at the same time, got rid of some possible rivals.

[48] The same rare verb is used in Num. xxv. 4 for an expiatory punishment, and the simple form is found in Gen. xxxii. 26 (EVV. 25): the hip of Jacob is 'dislocated'.

[49] The meaning of the end of the verse is obscure. The interpretation which I proposed in the fascicule of *Rois* in the *Bible de Jérusalem* is too weak. According to parallels, 'the great wrath' which falls upon the Israelites is a

11. *Human Sacrifices in Israel*

The foregoing inquiry has shown how exceptional had been human sacrifices among the earlier Semites, outside Phoenicia, and this conclusion prompts us to examine carefully the arguments which are adduced to prove that they had been practised in Israel and in the beginning considered lawful. As we said at the outset, certain historians of religion have held that the animal victim in a sacrifice had replaced a human victim: a man would not want to sacrifice himself, so he sacrificed his children, then in their place slaves or prisoners, and, finally, animals. In the same way too has been attempted the explanation of the origin of Israelite sacrifices: the animal would then be a substitute for the offerer, and this would be the significance of the imposition of the hand. In all forms of Israelite sacrifice the offerer laid his hand upon the head of the victim before it was offered, and this would signify that it was offered in his place.[50] This explanation is not exact, for there is no substitution of one victim for another. Every sacrifice implies a giving which deprives the offerer, and the abandonment to the divinity of some good to which he is essentially attached, which is a very part of himself,[51] and it is only this which is expressed by the rite of imposition of hand: the offerer thus shows that *this* victim is *his* victim, and that it is about to be sacrificed for his benefit and not in his place.[52] Admittedly there is a case where a rite which is similar outwardly brings about a transference: by an imposition of hands the scapegoat is laden with all the sins of the people; but it is not a sacrificial rite: precisely because of this transference the

divine wrath, and normally would be the wrath of Chemosh because it is to him that the sacrifice was offered: the Israelites are convinced of the efficacy of this extraordinary oblation, and fight shy of what might follow.

[50] Cf. R. Dussaud, *Les Origines cananéennes du sacrifice israélite* (1921), 2nd ed. (1941), p. 42: 'This rite has as its object the penetration of the animal by the soul of the offerer and making it a substitute for the individual. Hence the soul which will be poured out with the blood will be the very soul of the one who is offering sacrifice.'

[51] Cf. G. van der Leeuw, *Phänomenologie der Religion*² (1956), pp. 400–2.

[52] Cf. p. 28.

animal becomes unclean and is not sacrificed (Lev. xvi. 20–22). It would be quite arbitrary to conclude that in Israel animal sacrifices were the softened form of a primitive usage which would have required human victims.

Recently L. Rost asked whether the holocaust, which was rarely offered at the outset of Israelite history, might not have been at first a human sacrifice.[53] One can indeed instance the holocaust of Mesha's own son, of which we have spoken, and in Israel proper, the holocaust of which Isaac was the victim designate, and that of Jephthah's daughter. We shall come back to these two cases: they are exceptional, and it is not legitimate to look upon them as representative of the primitive type of holocaust. Suffice it to say that in a ritual of the Israelite type where the victims were either wholly burnt or burnt and eaten in part, a human sacrifice could not take any other form than that of a holocaust.

We must now examine in succession the texts of the historical books, of the Prophets, and of the Law wherein one finds or seems to find evidence of human sacrifices. The question is whether such sacrifices were really offered in Israel—we reply in the affirmative: and whether they were at some period or other of Yahwist religion accepted as lawful—we answer in the negative.

1. *Texts from the historical books*

The execution of prisoners of war cannot be looked upon as a sacrifice: it is the carrying out of a *ḥērem* or anathema which is a principle of the holy war[54] even if the execution is done 'before Yahweh': when Samuel executes Agag 'before Yahweh' (1 Sam. xv. 33) he is not offering him up in sacrifice, he is fulfilling the *ḥērem* which had been ordered (verse 3) and which Saul had not respected (verse 9).

We have shown that the Gibeonites when putting to death

[53] L. Rost, 'Erwägungen zum israelitischen Brandopfer', in *Von Ugarit nach Qumran* (*Festschrift Eissfeldt*) (1958), pp. 181–2; id., in *T.L.Z.* lxxxiii (1958), col. 331.

[54] *Ancient Israel: Its Life and Institutions*, pp. 260 f.

Saul's descendants (2 Sam. xxi. 1–14) followed a Canaanite ritual and not an Israelite one, and we have said that the death of the two sons of Hiel at Jericho (1 Kings xvi. 34) could be interpreted as other than a foundation sacrifice.

On the other hand a sure example of human sacrifice is the holocaust of Jephthah's daughter (Judges xi. 30–40). We must not water down the meaning of the text, as did certain Jewish and Christian commentators in the Middle Ages. Jephthah made a vow to Yahweh that he would offer as a holocaust the first person he was to meet if he returned a conqueror; this first person was his only daughter and he sacrificed her. The event was commemorated every year by a lamentation of the daughters of Israel (verse 40) and the narrative is calculated to give an explanation of this ceremony; it is a *hieros logos*. It has parallels in other literatures: in Crete a tale was told how Idomeneus, when caught in a storm, had vowed to sacrifice the first being he met on coming alongside the shore: it was his son.[55] In Asia Minor it was said that the river Meander owed its name to a certain Meander who had vowed, if victorious in war, to sacrifice the first person to come and congratulate him: it was his son, together with his mother and daughter; he offered them upon the altar, and then hurled himself into the river.[56] These parallels coming from regions relatively near Palestine and from a period not remote from that of the Judges (Idomeneus was returning from the war of Troy) do not mean that the narrative of Judges is just a story, but do mean that the idea of a vow bringing in its train the sacrifice of a human being was at that time accepted in the Near East. That this narrative explains a religious custom does not further prove it to be legendary: it is perfectly admissible that this custom, which was evidently limited to Gilead, Jephthah's home country, and which does not appear to have persisted, recalled a real event. This story is told with admirable simplicity. The redactor neither praises nor blames Jephthah

[55] Servius, *Aen.* iii. 121; xi. 264.

[56] Ps.-Plutarch, *De Fluviis*, ix. Other parallels have been collected by W. Baumgartner, 'Jephtas Gelübde', in *Archiv für Religionswissenschaft* xviii (1915), pp. 240–9.

and subsequent tradition did not condemn him (cf. Heb. xi. 32). Jephthah is a sincere Yahwist, he holds himself bound by the imprudent vow which he has made, for a vow is irrevocable—and his daughter thinks so too.[57] It is the expression of a religious conscience which is more primitive and more crude than that which is revealed in the two episodes which we singled out from the early days of Islam at Mecca, in which an analogous vow was commuted or declared invalid. Such objectivity on the part of the redactor does not prove that Jephthah's action was looked upon as legitimate, and the fact that it was commemorated serves to stress how much such a sacrifice was considered extraordinary. This passage cannot be used for determining the original character of holocausts, nor indeed for establishing a place for human sacrifices in the ancient ritual of Israel.[58]

There remains the sacrifice of Abraham (Gen. xxii).[59] It is often explained as an aetiological narrative which would explain and legitimize the substitution of an animal victim for a human victim. This is certainly not the meaning which the narrative has in the present general flow of the Genesis story. It tells, as the title in verse 1 suggests, of an unheard-of trial made of Abraham's obedience: he receives from God an order to sacrifice his only son, the son of promise on whom rests all the hope of the race. Just as the order to quit his country and his family (Gen. xii. 1) had cut Abraham off from his past, so this new

[57] Cf. Num. xxx. 3 (EVV. 2); Deut. xxiii. 22–24 (EVV. 21–23); Prov. xx. 25; Eccles. v. 3–5 (EVV. 4–6).

[58] Jephthah's antecedents seem to make foreign influence likely; his mother was not an Israelite, and he himself had lived outside Israel. Judges xi. 1–3.

[59] Amongst recent works cf. especially: A. George, 'Le Sacrifice d'Abraham. Essai sur les diverses intentions de ses narrateurs', in *Études de critique et d'histoire religieuses* (*Bibliothèque de la Faculté de Théologie Catholique de Lyon*, 2) (1948), pp. 99–110; D. Lerch, *Isaaks Opferung, christlich gedeutet* (1950), especially pp. 265–9; G. von Rad, *Das erste Buch Mose* (*Das Alte Testament Deutsch*) (1952), pp. 208–9. The latest contribution is that of Denise Piccard, 'Réflexions sur l'interprétation chrétienne de trois récits de la Genèse', in *Hommage à W. Vischer* (1960), pp. 183–7: we read there, p. 183, 'the theme which inspires [this story] goes back to a far-off period when the religion of nomad Semites included a human sacrifice alongside animal sacrifice'; according to all available evidence, the religion of the nomad Semites included nothing of the sort.

command cuts off his future. His obedience[60] is rewarded by a renewal of promises whose absolute gratuitousness is thus maintained. In the person of Isaac it was all Israel of the future which was bound upon the altar, and owed her survival only to the submission of her ancestor and the goodness of God to whom belongs the life of all, and who can claim this life of all and allow it to be in the freedom of His grace. Such are the narrative's profound purposes. It is not concerned with polemics against human sacrifices, nor with the legitimizing of a new rite in which an animal would have replaced a human victim. The narrative supposes however that in the milieu in which it took form human sacrifice was not an unknown thing, and it teaches, indirectly, that it is not thus that the God of Israel is honoured.

It is possible that before being embodied in the sequence of patriarchal history, this narrative, or the event which it relates, was linked to the foundation of a sanctuary. Abraham sets up an altar, offers a sacrifice, and gives a name to the place. Compare especially the narratives about the foundation of the sanctuary at Bethel by Jacob (Gen. xxviii. 10–21, xxxv. 1–7). Jacob gives the place a new name having reference to the religious experience which he underwent there, he anoints with oil the stele which he has set up and promises to pay the tithe, and then he comes back there on pilgrimage. The founder inaugurates the cult in the form in which it was to last: in fact pilgrimages were made to Bethel (1 Sam. x. 3) and tithes were paid there (Amos iv. 4). So too Genesis xxii may have been first of all the narrative of the foundation of a sanctuary where, from the outset, only animal victims were offered, in contrast with other, Canaanite, sanctuaries where human victims were also sacrificed. If this were so, this cult relationship was forgotten or veiled by the redactor of Genesis. The place of sacrifice, an essential element in a foundation narrative, remains unknown: Moriah is not a place but a country, and even the text is

[60] The 'fear of the Lord' (verse 12) is not, in the Old Testament, a fear of God; rather is it a submission to the orders and the will of God, cf. Job i. 1, 8.

uncertain, the Hebrew not being supported by any version;[61] the name which Abraham gives to the place, Yahweh-Yir'eh, corresponds to no known sanctuary.[62] Anyway only paradoxically could we use the narrative to establish that human sacrifices were ever legitimate in Israel; rather does it prove that human sacrifices were disapproved of and that this condemnation was put right back to the time of Abraham.

2. *Texts from the Prophets*

Apart from the texts which relate to sacrifices 'to Moloch', which we will treat of separately, allusions in the Prophets to human sacrifices are obscure. Hosea xiii. 2 is interpreted in this sense by many commentators.[63] The Hebrew text can in fact be translated: 'Sacrificers of men kiss calves', but the Hebrew text is not supported by the versions, and the resultant sense is not satisfactory. Verses 1–3 are an attack on the cult images of the Northern Kingdom, Jeroboam's calves, and it is hard to understand in this case a reference to human sacrifice. Hosea never speaks of it elsewhere, and there is no question of it anywhere in reference to the cults at Bethel and Dan. We had better draw no conclusions from this text, which is apparently corrupt.

In Micah vi. 1–8[64] Yahweh starts the court process of His people, recalling past benefits (verses 1–5); the people ask what is to be done to recover grace: 'Shall I present myself with

[61] The identification with the Temple hill at Jerusalem came late. 2 Chron. iii. 1.

[62] Gunkel, *Genesis* (1901), *in loco*, 'mit grosser Sicherheit' was for finding there the geographical term Yeruel (EVV. Jeruel), 2 Chron. xx. 16, and concluded that Gen. xxii was the sacred legend of the sanctuary of Yeruel, where at first children had been sacrificed. But the only text which mentions Yeruel refers to a region of the desert of Judah and not a particular locality, and there is no question of a sanctuary.

[63] Among the most recent, with or without correction of the text: Th. H. Robinson and F. Horst, *Die Zwölf Kleinen Propheten*[2] (1954), followed by J. Steinmann, *Le Prophétisme biblique des origines à Osée* (1959), p. 204; H. W. Wolff, *Dodekapropheton I, Hosea* (1961).

[64] The unity and antiquity of this passage have been contested but cf. A. Weiser, *Das Buch der Zwölf Kleinen Propheten I* (1949), which is the best recent commentary on this text, cf. also R. Hentschke, *Die Stellung der vorexilischen Schriftpropheten zum Kultus* (1957), pp. 104–7.

holocausts, with year old calves? Will Yahweh take pleasure in thousands of rams and the libation of torrents of oil? Shall I have to offer my first-born as the price of my misdeeds, the fruit of my womb for my own sin? (verses 6–7). But Yahweh demands nothing more than justice, love, and submission (verse 8). In their disarray, the people pass from possible offers to impossible offers, from ordinary holocausts to rams by thousands and torrential libations, and, to continue the progression, the last offer must appear even more impossible—the sacrifice of the first-born. We can conclude that such a kind of sacrifice was known, and, in the light of texts contemporary with Micah, we can read in this text a reference to sacrifices 'to Moloch', but we cannot conclude that such sacrifices were considered lawful: the prophet here rejoins the redactors of Genesis and, as we shall see, the prescriptions of the Law: Yahweh does not want human sacrifices.

The difficult passage in Isaiah lxvi. 3 draws up a parallel between four actions in legitimate worship and four actions in pagan worship:

> an ox is sacrificed, a man is killed;
> a lamb is slain, a dog is struck down;
> an offering is brought, swine-flesh is savoured;[65]
> incense memorial is made, idols are kissed.

The parallelism requires the killing of a man to be a religious action, as is that of the sacrifice of an ox.[66] The meaning, however, is not that he who sacrifices an ox does no better than he who sacrifices a man: the meaning is that he who does the one does the other too, and this syncretism is condemned. The passage dates from the return from Exile[67] and it is difficult to say what custom it refers to.[68]

[65] According to the correction proposed by Volz.

[66] Against A. Penna, *Isaia* (1958), *in loco*.

[67] I have discussed the interpretation and the date, 'Les Sacrifices de porcs en Palestine et dans l'Ancien Orient', in *Von Ugarit nach Qumran* (*Festschrift Eissfeldt*) (1958), pp. 263–5. Other references to recent literature can be found there.

[68] It is hardly likely that sacrifices 'to Moloch' continued so late.

The text of Ezekiel xx. 25–26 will be examined when dealing with the law of the first-born.

3. *The law of the first-born*

A certain number of critics find in the prescriptions relating to first-born children a decisive proof that human sacrifice was lawfully practised at the outset of Israel's history. The oldest legislative text is that of the Covenant Code (Exod. xxii. 28–29 (EVV. 29–30)), 'You will give Me the first-born of all your sons. You will do likewise with your small and large livestock. The first-born will stay seven days with his mother, and then on the eighth you will give him over to Me.' The prescription has the same absolute form in Exodus xiii. 2, 'Consecrate to Me every first-born, first-fruits of the mother's womb, from among the children of Israel, man or domestic animal, they are Mine.' But Exodus xiii. 11–15 and xxxiv. 19–20 order the buying back or redemption of the first-born of men, as does Numbers xviii. 15–16. According to Numbers iii. 40–51 and viii. 17–18 the Levites were given to Yahweh in place of the first-born who were due to him, and the children over and above the number of Levites at the time of the first numbering were redeemed.

Certain authors conclude that the laws which prescribe the buying back of the first-born are a mitigation of an ancient custom which imposed the sacrifice of them.[69] This is an arbitrary conclusion. The high esteem always attributed to the first-born—cf. already Genesis xlix. 3—makes it improbable.[70] On the

[69] J. G. Frazer, *The Golden Bough*² (1900), ii, pp. 43–59, especially p. 51; B. Stade, *Biblische Theologie des Alten Testaments I* (1905), p. 245; M. Jastrow, *Hebrew and Babylonian Traditions* (1914), pp. 29, 55; R. Dussaud, *Les Origines cananéennes du sacrifice israélite* (1921), 2nd ed. (1941), p. 167; A. Lods, *Israël des origines au milieu du VIIIe siècle* (1930), p. 330, E.T. by S. H. Hooke (1932), p. 286; E. Dhorme, *La Religion des Hébreux nomades* (1937), p. 33: 'primitive law is maintained in all its rigour in the book of Exodus xxii. 28–29'; O. Eissfeldt, *Molk als Opferbegriff* . . . (1935), p. 55, with reference to the same text: 'originally child sacrifices had a legitimate place in the cult of Yahweh'; the same author speaks more guardedly in the article 'Menschenopfer' in *R.G.G.*³ iv (1960), col. 868: a theoretical extension to the first-born of men of the law concerning animals, and from the beginning the buying back by an animal or by money was envisaged.

[*for footnote 70 see p. 71*

other hand Exodus xxxiv. 19–20, which prescribes the redemption of the first-born, belongs to the ancient Pentateuchal traditions and is not much antecedent to Exodus xxii. 28–29 (EVV. 29–30), which has an absolute formulation; Exodus xiii, which is posterior and composite, contains both together, the absolute order to consecrate without reservation all first-born men and animals (verse 2) and the precept of buying back the first-born of men (verse 13): the text thus passes from the general principle that all first-born belong to God to the different applications which are made of it for men and for animals. So, too, the 'Elohist' code of Exodus xxii abides by the principle[71] while the 'Yahwist' code of Exodus xxxiv makes explicit the different treatment accorded to the first-born of men. Comparison of the texts does not allow us to say that an ancient vigorous law has been subsequently modified. It would indeed be absurd to suppose that there could have been in Israel or among any other people, at any moment of their history, a constant general law, compelling the suppression of the first-born, who are the hope of the race.[72] So it is very difficult to admit that such a law existed in Israel even initially,[73] and 'there is no sure proof that there ever was in Israel a sacrifice of the first-born which was recognized as legitimate'.[74]

We must then explain Ezekiel xx. 25–26: 'I went to the point of giving them laws which were not good and customs which they could not live with, and I polluted them by their offerings, making them sacrifice all the first-born to punish them.'[75] The prophet seems to be saying not only that the sacrifice of the first-born has been, at one time, a general practice in Israel, but

[70] Thus J. Wellhausen, *Prolegomena zur Geschichte Israels*[3] (1886), p. 90; the commentaries of Baentsch (1900) and of Beer (1939), *in loco*.

[71] It cannot be explained by an allusion to circumcision, as is done by B. Couroyer, *L'Exode*[2] (1958), p. 23, n. *d*.

[72] Cf. M. Buber, *Königtum Gottes*[2] (1936), p. 219; W. Eichrodt, *Theologie des Alten Testaments I*[6] (1959), p. 89.

[73] H. Cazelles, *Études sur le code de l'alliance* (1946), p. 83.

[74] M. Noth, *Das zweite Buch Mose, Exodus* (1959), p. 80.

[75] The end of the verse 'so that they may know that I am Yahweh' is lacking in the Septuagint, and is an addition.

also that the practice was ordered by God. This meaning is impossible, first because history and common sense make it certain that Israel never sacrificed all her first-born, and secondly because Ezekiel elsewhere condemns the sacrifice of children (Ezek. xvi. 20–21), and again in the passage considered, a few verses further on (xx. 31).[76] To be understood, the passage must be kept in its context:[77] the whole chapter concerns the infidelities of Israel and their punishment. The laws of Yahweh are good and His customs are given to live by, but the people have profaned them (verses 11, 13, 21). Then Yahweh punishes them by laws which are not good and by customs impossible to live by: the sacrifice of the first-born. The prophet certainly refers to the law of Exodus xxii. 28–29 (EVV. 29–30); this law was good, it is the people who have made it bad by interpreting it in grossly materialistic ways and by following the errors of pagan neighbours. We can compare analogous formulae in St. Paul: the precept is good and right, but sin has laid hold of a good thing to bring about death (Rom. vii. 12–13); law intervened so that faults should be multiplied, but where sin has multiplied grace has more than abounded (Rom. v. 20). All the actions of men, even bad actions, enter into the plan of God, to whom they have a reference as to the first cause. In the same way God hardens hearts (Exod. iv. 21, vii. 3, &c.); He uses prophets to blind the people (Isa. vi. 9–10); He places in their mouth a lying spirit (1 Kings xxii. 18–23).

The opposite theme appears in the book of Jeremiah: 'They have built the high place of Topheth in the valley of Ben-Hinnom, to burn their sons and daughters, a thing which I had never prescribed and of which I had never thought' (Jer. vii. 31); 'they have built high places for Baal, to consume their sons in fire; this I have never prescribed nor ordered, never has it come

[76] This latter text is considered additional by W. Zimmerli, *Ezechiel, in loco*; the reasons he gives are not convincing.

[77] J. A. Bewer, *J.B.L.* lxxii (1953), pp. 159–61, gets round the difficulty by moving verse 27 and putting it as an introduction to verses 25–26; these would represent a blasphemy of the people, saying that God has given laws which were not good. The Targum went further: it is the people who have given themselves these bad laws.

to my thoughts' (Jer. xix. 5).[78] These passages reflect the same historical situation as that in Ezekiel: the practice of sacrificing children on the eve of the Exile; they refer to the scandalous misinterpretation of one single law, that of Exodus xxii. 28–29 (EVV. 29–30); but whereas Jeremiah says that this has never been the meaning of the law, Ezekiel says that Yahweh has allowed this corruption for the punishment of an unfaithful people.[79]

III. *Sacrifices 'to Moloch'*

The citations from Jeremiah introduce the subject of sacrifices 'to Moloch', which I have withheld till now. They do in fact constitute a special problem which has been very much discussed recently and which needed to be kept apart from the general problem of human sacrifices.

1. *Biblical texts*

The word 'Moloch' comes by medium of the Vulgate from Greek versions which thus transcribe the Hebrew *mōleḵ*. This noun occurs five times in the Holiness Code, which forbids the sacrifice of a son to Moloch (Lev. xviii. 21) and punishes it with death (Lev. xx. 2–5). It reappears in Jeremiah xxxii. 35[80] and in 2 Kings xxiii. 10: Josiah profaned the *tōpeṯ* of the valley of Ben-Hinnom so that no one should ever make his son or his daughter to pass through fire in honour of Moloch. The same name should be read in Isaiah xxx. 33, in place of *meleḵ*; conversely, in 1 Kings

[78] The two passages are attributed by the majority of critics to the editors of the book of Jeremiah; yet there seems to be no doubt that these parallel passages represent the authentic thought of the prophet, and are derived from one of his preachings, perhaps even in the very wording. Cf. A. Weiser, *Der Prophet Jeremia I* (1952), pp. 67, 74, and 168 f.). The theme is resumed a third time in Jer. xxxii, where verses 34–35 are an almost verbatim doublet of vii. 30–31.

[79] Against P. Volz, *Der Prophet Jeremia*[2] (1928), p. 204, according to whom Jeremiah did not yet consider the Code of the Covenant as inspired by God whereas Ezekiel looked upon it as a divine law which he tries to explain.

[80] A doublet of Jer. vii. 31 (cf. pp. 72 f., n. 78) to which is added the name of Moloch.

xi. 7, according to context and the versions, *Molek* should be corrected into *Milkom*, the national god of the Ammonites.

The most explicit text, that of 2 Kings xxiii. 10, allows us to discern references to the same cult in 2 Kings xvi. 3, xvii. 31, xxi. 6; Jeremiah vii. 31, xix. 5; Deuteronomy xii. 31, xviii. 10; Ezekiel xvi. 21, xx. 31, xxiii. 37 (sons or sons and daughters burnt in sacrifice); probably in Jeremiah ii. 23 (the 'valley' being that of Ben-Hinnom), Jeremiah iii. 24; and Psalms cvi. 37–38 (sons and daughters offered to idols).

According to Deuteronomy xii. 31 and xviii. 10 it is merely a pagan usage and Israelites must keep themselves clear of it; 2 Kings xvii. 31 charges with this practice the colonizers of Sepharvaim installed by the Assyrians in the former kingdom of Samaria; Isaiah xxx. 33 compares with this sacrifice the punishment which looms over Ashur. All the other texts are witness that the rite had really been practised by Israelites. The most explicit point out as the scene of this cult the valley of Ben-Hinnom, Gehenna, situated immediately south of Jerusalem, wherein was the *tōpeṯ* or 'incinerator',[81] which is briefly described in Isaiah xxx. 33. It would seem that the cult was not practised elsewhere; the only two historical references, 2 Kings xvi. 3 and xxi. 6, also bring us to Jerusalem. Ezekiel xxiii. 37–39 supposes that these sacrifices were offered outside the sanctuary yet in its neighbourhood, and it is understandable that the Holiness Code condemns them so roundly (Lev. xviii. 21, xx. 2–5), seeing that this Law is the work of Jerusalem priests, who, from the Temple, could see the smoke mounting up from the *tōpeṯ*. Thus this practice is geographically very much localized; and it is also very limited in time. Neither the sacrifice-to-be of Isaac, nor the death of the sons of Hiel at Jericho (if a sacrifice is really at issue), nor the holocaust of Jephthah's daughter, nor that of Mesha's son, from what we are told, are sacrifices of this kind. The first child whom we learn of as having been 'made to pass through the fire' is Ahaz's son (2 Kings xvi. 3); the first mention

[81] This meaning is justified by the Aramaic and Syriac, cf. the lexicon of Koehler–Baumgartner, s.v.

of the *tōpet* is in Isaiah xxx. 33, in an oracle pronounced at a time when Sennacherib was menacing Jerusalem. The reform of Josiah abolished this cult (2 Kings xxiii. 10), but it came to life again with seemingly renewed vigour after the failure of the reform: the Holiness Code was probably compiled between the promulgation of Deuteronomy and the Exile, the content of Jeremiah vii is attributed to the reign of Jehoiakim by the majority of commentators, and the prophecies of Ezekiel where this cult is mentioned reflect the religious situation in Judah just before the ruin of Jerusalem. Subsequently there are no more references to sacrifices to Moloch.[82]

The judgement of the Bible in their respect is unequivocal: they are always condemned, as much by Deuteronomy or the Deuteronomical redactor of Kings as by the priestly redactors of Leviticus and by the Prophets. They are reproved as being opposed to the will of Yahweh (Jer. vii. 31 and parallels), or as being offered to idols (Jer. ii. 23, iii. 24, xix. 5; Ezek. xvi. 20–21, xx. 31; Ps. cvi. 37–38), and as being done in imitation of those peoples whom God has disinherited from the Holy Land (Deut. xii. 29–31, xviii. 10; 2 Kings xvi. 3, xxi. 2 and 6).

Thus the Bible represents sacrifices to Moloch as an illegitimate practice which obtained in Jerusalem from the end of the eighth century to the beginning of the seventh century B.C., under the influence of Canaanite cults. We will now justify our conclusion, and give details about its origin.

2. *Molk sacrifices in the Carthaginian world*[83]

A certain number of Punic and Neo-Punic inscriptions from North Africa, engraved upon stelae which commemorated a

[82] I leave aside Isa. lvii. 5, because (1) these immolations of children in ravines, in clefts (or niches) of rock, have not the characteristics of sacrifices to Moloch; (2) the date of the passage is disputed: many exegetes place it before the Exile, others—and all those who maintain the unity of Trito-Isaiah—place it at the first period after the Return. O. Eissfeldt, *Einleitung in das Alte Testament*² (1956), p. 417, declares that both views are possible. The latest contributors to the study of the particular text of Isa. lvii. 5, M. Weiser, in *Z.A.W.* lxxii (1960), pp. 25–32, and J. C. Greenfield, ibid., lxxiii (1961), pp. 226–8, add nothing relevant to our question.

[83] I do not propose to take up the whole problem here. The data are set out

sacrifice, include the word *mlk*, alone or compounded with expressions the most remarkable of which are *mlk 'mr* and *mlk 'dm*. These inscriptions date roughly from the fourth to the first century B.C. The stelae are dedicated to Baal Hammon or to Baal Hammon and his associate Tanit. Some were found at Carthage, Guelma, and Susa, but the greater number come from El-Hofra near Constantine.[84]

The expression *mlk 'mr* only occurs four times in the North African inscriptions.[85] Its interpretation remained very uncertain until the discovery in 1930 at N'Gaous, 78 miles from Constantine, of several stelae, analogous but bearing a Latin inscription.[86] They date from the end of the second century or the beginning of the third century A.D., and they are dedications to Saturn, who is, in latinized Africa, the equivalent of Baal Hammon. The sacrifice offered is defined as a *molchomor*, which is evidently a transcription of the Punic *mlk 'mr*. Thus we can reckon *molk* as the vocalization of the first element.[87] O. Eissfeldt then showed that the word had a ritual sense, and he related it to the sacrifices of children in the Bible, which would have been not sacrifices offered to a god Moloch but a particular type of sacrifice which was called *molk*, as in Punic.[88] From another quarter, the meaning of the word *molk* has had

and discussed by H. Cazelles, art. 'Molok', in the *Supplément au dictionnaire de la Bible* v (1957), cols. 1337–46, unfortunately with errors in references. More recently: J. Hoftijzer, 'Eine Notiz zum punischen Kinderopfer', in *V.T.* viii (1958), pp. 288–92; J. G. Février, 'Essai de reconstruction du sacrifice Molek', in *J.A.* (1960), pp. 167–87.

84 A first lot had been found by L. Costa, about 1875; last publication by J. B. Chabot, *J.A.* (1917), pp. 50–72. A more important lot comes from the excavations of 1950, cf. A. Berthier and R. Charlier, *Le Sanctuaire punique d'El-Hofra à Constantine* (1955).

85 *C.I.S.* i. 307; Costa No. 58; Charlier Nos. 54 and 55.

86 Cf. especially J. Carcopino, 'Survivances par substitution des sacrifices d'enfants dans l'Afrique Romaine', in *R.H.R.* cvi (1932—B), pp. 592–9, taken up again in *Aspects mystiques de la Rome païenne* (1942), pp. 39–48.

87 J. G. Février, *J.A.* (1960), p. 168, proposes to read *molek* based on Charlier No. 54, which has *ml'k*: and the aleph would be a *mater lectionis*. It is more probable that it is but one of the orthographical variations which are so frequent in Punic.

88 O. Eissfeldt, *Molk als Opferbegriff im Punischen und Hebräischen und das Ende des Gottes Moloch* (1935). It will appear from what follows that today I would rewrite the review which I gave of it in *R.B.* lxv (1936), pp. 278–82.

light thrown on it by the Phoenician inscription at Karatepe, which gives a verb *hlk* in the *hiphil* (*yiphil* in Phoenician) employed in the sense of 'offer in sacrifice'.[89] The word *molk* would accordingly be a participial form and mean 'sacrificial offering'. As for the second element in the expression, *'mr*, the meaning of 'lamb' seems to impose itself because of the Assyrian *immeru*, Aramaic *'immar*, and by reason of the context and the stelae of N'Gaous, which when mentioning the *molchomor* speak explicitly about a lamb or display the representation of a lamb.[90]

In this 'offering of a lamb', the animal is a substitute. Three inscriptions from N'Gaous (out of five) say so clearly: *anima pro anima*, *sanguine pro sanguine*, *vita pro vita*, and two among them add *agnus pro vikario*.[91] This lamb is offered as a substitute for a child, whose name is given in four of the inscriptions which are fairly complete: there are two boys Impetratus,[92] Donatus, and two girls, both called Concessa. The names chosen are significant: then children had been asked for and obtained after the taking of a vow, *ex voto* say the inscriptions. The vicarious sacrifice of the lamb satisfies the vow. However, we should not be hasty in putting back to the Punic period all the data which can be drawn from Latin inscriptions of the second and third centuries A.D. Child sacrifices had by then been severely forbidden by the Romans, and though they were still secretly offered,[93] substitution had become the normal practice. Yet this substitution was already being effected at an early period: R. Dussaud read *mlk 'mr* on a stele from Malta of the seventh or sixth century B.C.[94]

The expression *mlk 'dm* is much more frequent.[95] There are

[89] A. Alt in *Die Welt des Orients* i (1947–52), pp. 282–3, followed by J. G. Février, *R.H.R.* cxliii (1953—B), p. 9; cf. *J.A.* (1955), p. 53. This resolves a doubt which I had expressed in *R.B.* xlv (1936), p. 280.

[90] M. Buber, *Königtum Gottes*² (1936), p. 214, objects that the transcription should be *immor* or *emmor*, but the objection is not fatal, as he himself admits.

[91] The expression recurs also in Stele I, according to a new reading of Berthier and Charlier, cf. *Karthago* iv (1953), p. 6.

[92] Stele I, following the reading of Berthier and Charlier.

[93] Tertullian, *Apol.* ix.

[94] This the Stele *C.I.S. I* 123*b*, cf. R. Dussaud, *C.R.A.I.* (1946), pp. 376–7.

[95] One inscription from Althiburos, four inscriptions from Constantine (old

various interpretations. Eissfeldt recognizes that it can be translated 'sacrifice of a man', but he prefers to read it as 'sacrifice offered by a man' of the people, i.e. who is neither priest nor king.[96] Dussaud accepts this last rendering;[97] Février defends the translation 'sacrifice of blood',[98] and other interpretations are offered by those who refuse to see a sacrificial meaning in *molk*.[99] It is tempting to keep to the simplest of these senses: 'sacrifice of a man' or 'human sacrifice',[100] *'dm* in Hebrew standing for men as opposed to animals. *Mlk 'dm* 'sacrifice of a man' would thus be contrasted with *mlk 'mr* 'sacrifice of a lamb'. The uncertainty of this translation should be resolved by the words which frequently follow *mlk 'dm*, and which should explain and clarify the expression: *bsrm btm*, and variant spellings. These words are unfortunately very obscure. Bilingual, Latino-Punic, inscriptions of Tripolitania seem to establish an equivalence between *btm* and *pro pecunia sua*,[101] but the precise force of the term in Punic is probably 'integrally', 'totally'. As for *bsrm*, now that *-m* is well established to be the suffix of the third person singular,[102] I would less hesitantly translate 'his flesh' in the sense of 'his child'. The complete expression would then mean 'a human sacrifice, his own child, totally'.[103]

excavations), thirteen from Constantine (new excavations = Charlier Nos. 28–32 and 33–41).

[96] *Molk als Opferbegriff* . . ., pp. 19–20.

[97] *C.R.A.I.* (1946), p. 380, n. 3.

[98] By admitting a prosthetic *aleph* in *'dm*, *R.H.R.* cxliii (1953—B), p. 11; *J.A.* (1960), p. 180.

[99] M. Buber, *Königtum Gottes*² (1936), pp. 214–15: *mlk 'mr* = 'The Malk has spoken'; *mlk 'dm(n)* = 'The Malk is Lord'. This wins the approval of W. Kornfeld, *W.Z.K.M.* li (1948–52), pp. 287–92; R. Charlier, *Karthago* iv (1953), pp. 3–48, accepts the explanation of *mlk 'mr*, but for *mlk 'dm* he suggests 'the king of the earth' or 'the lord of humanity'.

[100] Cf. J. Hoftijzer, *V.T.* viii (1958), pp. 288–92. R. Dussaud objected, *C.R.A.I.* (1946), p. 380, n. 3, that only children were sacrificed, but the expression can equally well be applied to children, as is proved by the Latin texts of classical authors relating to these Punic sacrifices—*humana victima*, Pliny, *Nat. Hist.* xxxvi. 39; *humanas hostias*, Lactantius, *Div. Inst.* i. 21; *homines ut victimas immolabant*, Justin (T. Pompeius), XVIII. vi. 2.

[101] Cf. Levi della Vida, 'Iscrizioni neopuniche di Tripolitania', in *Rendiconti dell'Accademia dei Lincei* (1949), pp. 400–5; id., *Africa Italiana* vi, p. 107.

[102] J. Friedrich, *Z.D.M.G.* cvii (1957), pp. 290–2; already J. G. Février, *J.A.* (1951), p. 6.

[103] Thus J. Hoftijzer, *V.T.* viii (1958), p. 292.

Uncertainties manifestly remain. One conclusion seems established: *molk*, in Punic, is a ritual term used of the sacrifices of children, for whom it was admitted an animal victim could be substituted.

On the sacrifice of children at Carthage we have numerous literary attestations, both Greek and Latin; nearly all link them explicitly with the cult of Saturn-Kronos, i.e. Baal Hammon. I will only refer to the principal texts. According to Quintus Curtius[104] the practice dated from the foundation of Carthage and lasted up to the destruction of the city. According to Plutarch,[105] Gelon of Syracuse, second century B.C., imposed upon the Carthaginians who had been conquered the obligation of giving up these immolations of children to Kronos. If there was an interlude, it did not last long. According to Diodorus Siculus,[106] Hamilcar offered his child to Kronos according to the age-old rite. Tertullian[107] attests that in the proconsulate of Tiberius, priests of Saturn who went in for these sacrifices were crucified; yet these sacrifices continued in secret.

Two texts are more detailed. The first is from Plutarch:[108]

> The Carthaginians were wont to slaughter their own children at the foot of altars. Those who had no children would buy some little ones from poor folk, and slaughter these as one does with lambs or birds. The mother would be present at the sacrifice, never shedding a tear nor uttering a groan. Nevertheless at the base of the statue, the whole arena was filled with flute-players and drummers, so that the cries and screams of the victims should not be heard.

The second text from Diodorus Siculus is even more important.[109] In 310 B.C. the Carthaginian army was crushed by Agathocles of Syracuse. Thereupon the Carthaginians

> deemed that Kronos too was hostile to them; the reason being that aforetime they sacrificed to this god the best of their children, whereas

[104] *Hist.* IV. iii. 23.
[105] *Ser. Num. Vind.* 6.
[106] *Bibl. Hist.* XIII. lxxxvi. 3.
[107] *Apol.* ix. 2–4. The Tiberius referred to is either the Emperor Tiberius acting in the Provinces in virtue of his proconsular power, or else an unknown proconsul of the second century.
[108] *De Superst.* xiii. 171*d*.
[109] *Bibl. Hist.* XX. xiv. 4–6.

subsequently they had begun to buy children secretly and nourish them and send them off to the sacrifice. Inquiry revealed that certain of the children sacrificed had been substituted. Thinking over these things and seeing the enemy encamped before the walls, they were filled with a religious fear at the idea of having made nothing of the honours traditionally due to the gods. They hastened to put these errors right, and decreed the public sacrifice of two hundred children chosen from the most distinguished families; other citizens, who were the objects of accusations, voluntarily offered their own children, no less than three hundred.

They had among them a bronze statue of Kronos with outstretched hands, palms uppermost, yet inclined towards the ground, so that the child who was placed in these palms would roll off and fall into a pit filled with fire.

This sacrifice of two hundred high-born children after the defeat inflicted by Agathocles is also mentioned by Lactantius,[110] who says that he holds it from Pescennius Festus (an author otherwise unknown). The manner of sacrifice is confirmed by Clitarchus, quoted by one of Plato's scholiasts:[111] Phoenicians and particularly Carthaginians would vow their children to Kronos; there was a bronze statue of Kronos whose hands were extended over a bronze brazier in which the child was burnt. The two texts are not contradictory. The brazier of Clitarchus was placed in the pit mentioned by Diodorus.

These are the texts which have provided the rabbis with their material for a description of a statue of Moloch, which would have stood in the valley of Ben-Hinnom.[112] This Jerusalem statue is a rabbinic fancy, but there is no reason to doubt that in Carthage this statue, which Diodorus and Clitarchus describe and Plutarch mentions, really existed. Only one remark should be added: contrary to the conception which the rabbis imposed on medieval and modern commentators, this statue does not

[110] *Div. Inst.* i. 21.

[111] Schol. Plat. *Rep.* 337A in edition of Didot, iii, p. 321, or F. Jacoby, *F. Gr. Hist.*, 11 B, No. 137. The same thing in the lexicons of Suidas and Photius, s.v. σαρδάνιος γέλως or σαρδόνιος γέλως.

[112] G. F. Moore, 'The Image of Moloch', in *J.B.L.* xvi (1897), pp. 161–5; O. Eissfeldt, *Molk als Opferbegriff . . .*, pp. 66–71.

constitute the furnace itself: that is the pit—with or without a gridiron—into which the victim fell after being placed on the extended hands of the idol. These ancient authorities are only speaking about Carthage and it is not necessary to suppose that such a staging took place wherever these sacrifices were offered in the Punic regions.

The essential point is that the victim was burnt. It has been granted that it was burnt alive,[113] yet the only text that can be invoked is that of Clitarchus, who speaks about this sacrifice in the context of the 'sardonic smile': he says that the victims 'died laughing' as their mouths opened when the flame reached them. Apart from this questionable authority, all the other texts recognize a slaughtering of the child before falling into the fire, and some say so explicitly.[114]

Archaeology also throws light on these sacrifices. A stele from Carthage shows a priest carrying a child in his arms just as other priests carry their victim.[115] Excavation in the sanctuary of Susa (the ancient Adrumetum) has unearthed a pit similar to that spoken of by Diodorus and where victims were burnt: 'A space of four square metres, at the S.E. end of the excavation, was void of all stelae and was at this level completely burnt. Beneath this plot all the earth and all that it contained was calcined and reduced to an ash-like state by the heat of the braziers. The paths leading to it were also lacking in stelae.'[116] Where the

[113] In line with S. Gsell, *Histoire ancienne de l'Afrique du Nord IV* (1920), p. 410.

[114] This has been well established by J. Guey, *Mélanges d'archéologie et d'histoire (Rome)* liv (1937), pp. 94–99. This conclusion is accepted by J. G. Février, who has attempted an 'Essai de reconstitution du sacrifice molek', in *J.A.* (1960), pp. 167–87.

[115] L. Poinssot and R. Lantier, 'Un Sanctuaire de Tanit à Carthage', in *R.H.R.* lxxxvii (1923), i, pl. iv. 2, and better in G. Charles-Picard, *Les Religions de l'Afrique antique* (1954), p. 45, fig. 4.

[116] P. Cintas, *Revue Africaine* (1947), pp. 34 f. These sacrifices were not limited to northern Africa, but were also offered in the Punic dependencies of the Mediterranean. We have referred to the Maltese inscription which tells of a *mlk 'mr*. Some excavations have revealed urns and stelae similar to those of Susa: at Nora in Sardinia, cf. G. Patroni, 'Nora, colonia fenicia in Sardegna', in *Monumenti Antichi* xiv (1904), cols. 110–258, especially cols. 157–65; at Sulcis, G. Lilliu, 'Le Stele puniche di Sulcis (Cagliari)', ibid. xl. 3 (1944), cols. 293–418; a more general study is G. Pesce, *Sardegna punica*

stelae have not been found stacked up in a *favissa* as at El-Hofra, they indicate that urns are buried at their base; the urns contain calcinated bones which are the remains of a sacrifice.

It had been already pointed out that some of these bones were those of young children. Quite recently a technical study of these deposits was made by Dr. J. Richard.[117] He examined the contents of 180 urns, of which 42 came from the sanctuary of Salammbo at Carthage, and the remainder from the sanctuary of Susa. Out of this number, 88 urns contained human bones of one, two, or several children; 59 contained human bones mixed with lambs' bones; 29 contained lambs' bones only (4 had too little content to allow of any diagnosis). The fact that there is never any complete skeleton, that there are often remains of several individuals, and that they are often mixed with animal bones indicates that they have been drawn from a common pyre. Still, the number of urns examined corresponds roughly to the number of victims as calculated from the bone remains. This would seem to indicate that each urn and each stele served to recall a particular sacrifice. Various methods were used to determine the age of the children. Average percentages work out as follows: 6 per cent. were prematurely born children, 74 per cent. were newly born, 20 per cent. were a few months old or more, some up to 3 and 4 years old.

Besides bones, the urns contained sandy soil, cinders and coniferous charcoal, land and sea shells, and the bones of small mammals: the urns were filled from the pit which was dug into the sand and where the pyre was laid out. There were also a few ornaments which had been worn by children of wealthier families.

(1961), pp. 68 f., 85 f.; in Sicily at Motya, cf., most recently, B. S. J. Isserlin, in *Illustrated London News*, 3 March 1962, cols. 328–30. Excavations are continuing at Sulcis and at Motya. One can only hope that the content of the urns will be the object of a study analogous to that which was made at Carthage and Susa.

[117] *Étude médico-légale des urnes sacrificielles puniques et leur contenu. Thèse pour le Doctorat en médecine.* Institut Médico-Légal de Lille (1961). I thank Dr. J. Richard for letting me have a copy of this thesis.

Chronologically the proportion of human bones and animal bones would be set out thus:[118]

Period I (eighth and seventh centuries)	
human bones alone	55·5%
animal bones alone	11·1%
mixed	33·3%
Period II (sixth and fifth centuries)	
human bones alone	48%
animal bones alone	23%
mixed	29%
Period III (fourth to second century)	
human bones alone	21·7%
animal bones alone	26%
mixed	52·2%

The proximity of urns containing human bones and urns containing animal bones, and the mingling of the two kinds of bones in the same urns, forces us to recognize that all these deposits refer to the same cult. This is the one we have described and which comprised child sacrifices and the sacrifices of animals substituted for some children. If the chart of frequencies drawn up by Dr. Richard holds good, it allows for some important conclusions. The figures indicate, firstly, that the practice of substitution goes back to the beginning of Carthage's history. This was already suggested by the stele from Malta (seventh–sixth century B.C.) on which was read *mlk 'mr*; and secondly they indicate that sacrifices of children continued at least to the destruction of Carthage; which is what Quintus Curtius already said.[119] Note, however, that the percentage of urns containing human bones alone is consistently going down, while the percentage of urns containing animal bones alone is consistently going up.

[118] These divisions were established by J. Richard on the basis of the types of urns, following in this P. Cintas, *Céramique punique* (1950). It seems that he was not able to take into consideration the archaeological levels from which these urns come; the picture he presents may be qualified by the uncertainty that clings to the date of the foundation of Carthage, and our still limited knowledge of the evolution of Punic ceramics. Yet the conclusions we can draw from it remain valid.

[119] Cf. n. 104.

Both archaeology and written texts compel us to recognize that the sacrifices of children were a current practice in the cult of Baal Hammon in North Africa, and that they were kept up for a very long time. One last point remains to be made. These sacrifices are commonly looked upon as an offering of the first-born, but this view has no basis. The stelae of N'Gaous, on which out of four children who are named two are girls, serve to show that at least it is not a matter of first-born male children only; and the texts from the classical authors use indifferently παῖδες, παιδία, τέκνα, 'children', without determination of sex. There is no literary text and no inscription which speaks of the 'first-born'.[120]

3. *Sacrifices of children in Phoenicia*

These Punic sacrifices were a heritage of the Phoenician country of origin. Quintus Curtius says so explicitly when speaking of the siege of Tyre by Alexander:

> Some were counselling the resumption of a rite which I cannot believe to be pleasing to the gods, and which had been in abeyance for centuries, I mean the sacrifice to Saturn of a child of freeborn family. This rite, sacrilegious rather than sacred, was transmitted by its founders to Carthage, where, it is said, it was practised up to the destruction of the city. And if the counsel of the elders who held authority had not intervened, a barbarous superstition would have triumphed over humane principles.[121]

On his side, Porphyry writes:

> In the great catastrophes which follow upon wars, drought, and plague, the Phoenicians would mark out one of their dear children to be sacrificed to Kronos. The History of Phoenicia which Sanchuniaton composed in Phoenician, and which Philo of Byblos translated into Greek in eight books, is full of such sacrifices.[122]

The text is taken up by Eusebius,[123] who adds, also from Philo

[120] Cf. J. Carcopino, *R.H.R.* cvi (1932—B), p. 599, and *Aspects mystiques de la Rome païenne*, p. 47; J. G. Février, *J.A.* (1960), pp. 177–9.

[121] Quintus Curtius, *Hist.* IV. iii. 23, trans. H. Bardon in the Budé Collection; but one *lapsus* needs to be corrected: Neptune has taken the place of Saturn.

[122] Porphyry, *De Abstinentia*, ii. 56.

[123] Eusebius, *Praep. Ev.* iv. 16. 6; cf. *Orat. pro Const.* 13.

of Byblos, that these sacrifices were accomplished in a manner full of mystery, and that the rite had been inaugurated by Kronos himself who thus sacrificed his son.[124] Philo was long suspected of having invented an ancient Phoenician author, a Sanchuniaton who was thought to have lived before the Trojan war, so as to give authority to his own compositions. Ras Shamra texts, however, have proved him right and corroborated much of the information which he gives.[125] So we can admit that sacrifices of children obtained in older days among the Phoenicians, and Quintus Curtius tells us that they were still practised at the time of the foundation of Carthage, but that they had ceased to be, at least officially, several centuries before the conquest of Alexander.[126]

Unfortunately, Philo does not describe the rite that was followed. He merely says that it took place 'in a mysterious way', and if we are to see in it the ritual by fire of the Punic sacrifices, we must rely on Quintus Curtius who says that Carthage had long maintained a custom which she held from her founders.[127] Having admitted this equivalence, we must now try to determine whether this type of sacrifice was termed *molk* in Phoenicia as it was at Carthage.

Mlk never appears with a sacrificial meaning in the Phoenician inscriptions, but this silence is explicable by reason of the rarity and the character of inscriptions earlier than the sixth century, when these sacrifices, as we have just said, were no longer offered. But we have the Ras Shamra texts which hail from the same religious milieu and include liturgical texts which go back to the fourteenth century, or approximately the period in which Philo places Sanchuniaton. What information we can get from

[124] Ibid. iv. 16. 11; cf. i. 10. 45. These fragments of Philo of Byblos are edited in Müller, *F.H.G.* iii, p. 570, fragments 3 and 4; Jacoby, *F. Gr. Hist.*, No. 790, fr. 3 (3–4).

[125] Cf. O. Eissfeldt, articles 'Philo Byblius' and 'Sanchunjaton', in *R.G.G.*^{3} v (1961), cols. 346–7 (with bibliography) and 1361.

[126] O. Eissfeldt, *Ras Schamra und Sanchunjaton* (1939), pp. 69–70, concludes from this that these sacrifices ceased in Phoenicia in the seventh century B.C. at the same period in which Deuteronomy (and, I add, the Holiness Code) protested against sacrifices 'to Moloch' in Israel.

[127] Loc. cit.; cf. also Clitarchus, cited above, p. 80, n. 111: 'The Phoenicians and specially the Carthaginians'.

these for our subject is very slender. In what seems to be a ritual, *mlk* appears three times[128] but in a context full of lacunae. C. H. Gordon recognizes in it a type of sacrifice which he relates to the Hebrew *mōleḵ*.[129] He adds to it another text which enumerates sacrifices to various gods and in which *mlk* comes between two words which defy interpretation;[130] a feminine form *mlkt* appears to be found in a third text which is too mutilated to be usable.[131] Anyway it would be strange that the name of the same sacrifice should have a masculine and a feminine form. It would be stranger still that the two forms *mlk* and *mlkt* both designating this sacrifice should be found in the same line of the Poem of the Gracious Gods and Fair, as Cazelles seems inclined to admit;[132] it is much more likely that these words have their ordinary sense of 'king' and 'queen'.[133]

Available evidence has recently been enhanced by a new text. Among the first alphabetic tablets discovered in 1929 was found a list of divinities in which, at the end, was mentioned *mlkm*, which Gordon vocalized as Milkom.[134] A tablet from the excavation of 1956 contains the same list in syllabic Akkadian;[135] *mlkm* is represented by 'the Mâliks' (plural form). It would be easy to see in this the god Mâlik who is vouched for in the Mesopotamian pantheon, although in a secondary rank.

[128] **3.** 48, 50, 53. I follow Gordon's numbering. A copy of this ritual, more complete, was found in 1954 and published by Mlle Herdner in *Syria* xxxiii (1956), pp. 104–12. It throws no decisive light on our problem. Mlle Herdner admits that *mlk* 'might well designate a sacrifice (hebr. molek)', p. 112.

[129] C. H. Gordon, *Ugaritic Manual* (1955), glossary No. 1119. In his *Ugaritic Literature* (1949), he translates it as 'king'.

[130] **9.** 10.

[131] **41.** 4. The sacrificial sense is however accepted by J. G. Février, *J.A.* (1955), p. 53.

[132] **52.** 7; H. Cazelles, art. 'Molok', *Supplément au dictionnaire de la Bible* v, col. 1345.

[133] Thus C. H. Gordon, *Ugaritic Literature* (1949); R. Largement, *La Naissance de l'Aurore* (1949); G. R. Driver, *Canaanite Myths and Legends* (1956); J. Aistleitner, *Die mythologischen und kultischen Texte aus Ras Schamra* (1959). Others recognize in it a verbal form 'to rule'. Thus C. Virolleaud, *Syria* xiv (1933); Th. H. Gaster, *Thespis* (1950).

[134] **17.** 11; *Ugaritic Literature*, p. 108.

[135] Cf. J. Nougayrol, *C.R.A.I.* (1957), pp. 82 f.; E. Weidner, *A.f.O.* xviii (1957), p. 170; the text itself is not yet published.

But the plural is strange, and these *mlkm* come among a group of cult objects or actions which are divinized, after a god Censer and a god Lyre and before a god *Šlm*, which could be the *Šlm* sacrifice, the communion sacrifice of the Bible, but which the Akkadian version represents by *Salimu*, which could be a divine name.[136] It is still possible that the *mlkm* gods are divinized *molk* sacrifices and that the Akkadian vocalization is incorrect.

Both about the name which child sacrifices received in Phoenicia and about the rite observed in these, the indigenous texts leave us uncertain.

4. *Molk sacrifices and sacrifices 'to Moloch'*

Paradoxically, it is the Bible which enables us to forge a link between Phoenicia and Carthage. For indeed the sacrifices 'to Moloch' follow the same ritual as that used in child sacrifices in Punic regions. The little victims were 'passed through the fire', that is to say burnt, as at Carthage, and Ezekiel xvi. 21[137] shows that they were first of all slaughtered, as we have established for North Africa. Diodorus Siculus tells us that the children fell into a pit full of fire, and such a pit has been found in the excavations at Susa. It is in this way that we should picture to ourselves the *tōpeṯ* of the valley of Ben-Hinnom: according to Jeremiah

[136] Cf. H. Cazelles, *Biblica* xxxviii (1957), pp. 485–6.

[137] Cf. also Ezek. xxiii. 37–39 (verse 38, which breaks the run of the passage, is probably an explanation of verse 39). The mention of 'prostitutions' of Israel in the two contexts of Ezekiel provides an apparent ground for the hypothesis of K. Elliger, *Z.A.W.* lxvii (1955), p. 17: according to this author, the explanation of the insertion of Lev. viii. 21 (sacrifices to Moloch) in a series of laws on sexual relationships is that children born of sexual unions associated with impure cults were thus sacrificed; W. Zimmerli, *Ezechiel*, fasc. 5 (1958), on Ezek. xvi. 20 judges this hypothesis plausible. It is however contradicted by the only historical examples which are given to us, 2 Kings xvi. 3, xxi. 6, unless we say that the son of Ahaz and that of Manasseh were the fruit of such unions, which we could not easily admit. In Ezekiel 'prostitution' means disorder in worship generally, as is commonly the case in the Prophets. The mention of these sacrifices in the context of Lev. xviii remains strange. Perhaps it is to be explained by the composite character of the Code of Holiness, and by the parallel of Lev. xx, where the condemnation of the sacrifices 'to Moloch' (verses 2–5) comes before a series of laws (verses 10–21) very much like those of Lev. xviii.

vii. 32,[138] 'burials will be made at Topheth, for lack of space', i.e. the place of wicked sacrifices will become a common grave. More explicit is the text of Isaiah xxx. 33: the prophet announces the defeat of Assyria, 'for a long time back his *tōpeṯ* has been prepared—he too is for the *mōleḵ*—a deep and wide hearth, straw and wood in plenty there; the breath of Yahweh, like a torrent of sulphur, is about to fire it all'.[139] The identity of the rites practised in Israel and at Carthage can only be explained in terms of a common source, which is evidently Phoenicia. Despite the laconism of the texts, we must admit that these same rites were practised there. It thus becomes more likely that they had the same name as at Carthage: they were *molk* sacrifices.

Must we then conclude that this sacrifice was also called *molk* in Israel, and are we to understand, in the texts which we have cited, that the Israelites gave over their children for a '*molk* sacrifice' and not in honour of a god Molek? Does this mean the end of the god 'Moloch'? Such, we will recall, was Eissfeldt's thesis.[140]

The problem is more complicated than would appear. For indeed *Melek*, 'the king', is a divine appellative which enters into the composition of many Phoenician and Hebrew names, where it changes places with proper names of divinities.[141] This appellative is found again under the forms *muluk* and *malik* in the name lists of Mari at the beginning of the second millenary B.C.[142] Further, Mâlik is the proper name of a god of the Mesopotamian pantheon known from the third millenary,[143] and we have seen that it was thus that Akkadian

[138] With the doublet of Jer. xix. 6 and 11*b*.

[139] The text is uncertain, cf. the commentaries. I translate by 'hearth' the word *m^eḏûrāh*, which is only found again in Ezek. xxiv. 9, in conjunction with wood and fire. But it is not a heap of wood or 'pyre'. According to its etymology, the *m^eḏûrāh* is round, and according to our text, hollowed out. It is a pit in which a fire is made, a hearth. This is consonant with the text of Ezekiel.

[140] Cf. p. 76, n. 88.

[141] Cf. *R.B.* xlv (1936), p. 281; lxii (1955), p. 610.

[142] G. Dossin, *R.A.* xxxv (1938), p. 178, n. 1; H. Cazelles, *Supplément au dictionnaire de la Bible* v, col. 134 n.

[143] H. Cazelles, loc. cit., with the references.

transcribed *mlk* in the list of divinities of Ras Shamra.[144] Finally, remember that the Ammonites, immediate neighbours of the Israelites, had Milkom as their national god.

On the other hand, the only indication which the Bible gives about the practice of these sacrifices outside Israel is in connexion with the colonizers from Sepharvaim, in Syria, who had been installed in Samaria, and who burnt their children in honour of their gods Adrammelek and Anammelek, 2 Kings xvii. 31. Adrammelek is a corruption of Adadmelek, whose cult is attested at Tell Ḥalâf in northern Syria at the beginning of the first millenary:[145] it is Adad the King, and we have cited two texts from Tell Ḥalâf which speak of children 'burnt before Adad'.[146]

Returning to the biblical texts which mention 'Moloch' we find that all can be interpreted as if *mōleḵ* was a divine name, and that some can with difficulty be interpreted otherwise: when Leviticus xx. 5 condemns those who 'prostitute themselves following Molek' we have a divinity and not a type of sacrifice.[147] This sense is confirmed by the texts which, without citing Molek, consider that these sacrifices are offered to idols.

Our conclusion will be delicately balanced. It is certain that these sacrifices 'to Moloch' are identical with the *molk* sacrifices of North Africa, and that they are, in Israel, something borrowed from the Phoenicians. It is likely that in Phoenicia these sacrifices were also called *molk*. But it appears that already at the time of borrowing the word was not understood, and that the Israelites

[144] Cf. p. 86, n. 135, and p. 87, n. 136.

[145] Cf. A. Pohl, *Biblica* xxii (1941), pp. 35–37; O. Eissfeldt, *Mélanges Isidore Lévy* (*Annuaire de l'Institut de Philologie et d'Histoire Orientales et Slaves* xiii) (1955), pp. 153 f. On all this question cf. W. F. Albright, *Archaeology and the Religion of Israel*² (1946), pp. 162–4.

[146] Cf. pp. 59 f., n. 41. Cf. the more recent Assyrian text cited on p. 59, n. 35: the eldest son will be burnt in the sacred precinct of Adad.

[147] These arguments, and others of unequal value, have been adduced by recent authors who do not accept or only partly accept Eissfeldt's thesis; cf. particularly W. Kornfeld, 'Der Moloch', in *W.Z.K.M.* li (1948–52), pp. 287–313; K. Dronkert, *De Molochdienst in het Oude Testament* (1953); E. Dhorme, 'Le Dieu Baal et le Dieu Moloch', in *Anatolian Studies* vi (1956), pp. 57–61; J. Gray, *The Legacy of Canaan* (Supplement to *V.T.* v) (1957), p. 126; W. Zimmerli, *Ezechiel*, fasc. 5 (1958), on Ezek. xvi. 20.

thought that these sacrifices were destined for a king-god, a Melek, like Adrammelek or Anammelek, for whom at the same period children were burnt at Samaria.[148] Anyway, it is evident that this custom, brought in from outside, limited to the region of Jerusalem, restricted in time and condemned by all who stood for Yahwism, cannot prove that human sacrifices were ever lawful in Israel.

[148] But this rite did not come into Israel through the medium of the colonizers of Samaria. The first historic example is the sacrifice of Ahaz's son, and thus before the fall of Samaria, if we go by the most acceptable chronology for the end of the reign of Ahaz.

IV

EXPIATORY SACRIFICES

BECAUSE sacrifice is a homage to God and establishes or re-establishes good relations between God and those who are faithful to Him, so, too, sacrifice appeases the anger of God against the sinner and averts punishment. For this reason every sacrifice has an expiatory force. After the plague which was in punishment of David's sin, he then offered holocausts and communion sacrifices: 'Then Yahweh had pity on the country and the scourge drew aside from Israel', 2 Samuel xxiv. 25. But there are sins so grave that sacrifice cannot expiate them, as was the sin of the sons of Eli: 'That is why—I swear it to the house of Eli—neither sacrifice, *zeḇaḥ*, nor offering, *minḥāh*, will ever wipe out the faults of the house of Eli', 1 Samuel iii. 14. But an awareness of the fault committed and the need to be restored to grace before God brought about the institution of special rites, of expiatory sacrifices.

Almost half the sacrificial code of the Second Temple is consecrated to them (Lev. iv–v, vi. 17–vii. 10, to which must be added Lev. x. 16–20). The ritual has no common term to designate expiatory sacrifices and speaks in succession or at once of two sorts of sacrifice: the sacrifice for sin, *ḥaṭṭā'ṯ*, and the sacrifice of reparation, *'āšām*. Despite the fullness of the texts, it remains difficult to determine the proper meaning of each and the reason for their being distinct.

1. *Sacrifice for Sin*[1]

The Hebrew word *ḥaṭṭā'ṯ* means all at once the sin, the sacrifice which deletes it, and the victim of such a sacrifice. The ritual

[1] For a general consideration of expiatory sacrifices cf. A. Médebielle, *L'Expiation dans l'Ancien et le Nouveau Testament*, i. *L'Ancien Testament*

is contained in Leviticus iv. 1–v. 13, vi. 17–23. The victim varies according to the status of the wrongdoer: an ox is offered for the sin of the 'anointed priest', the high-priest,[2] whose culpability sullies the whole people, an ox also for the sin of the people, a he-goat for the sin of the 'prince', *nāśī'*, the title given to the leader of the community in Ezekiel's plan (Ezek. xliv–xlvi), and effectively borne by Sheshbazzar (Ezra i. 8), a goat or a sheep for the sin of an individual (Lev. iv. 3–35). Poor people can replace these costly offerings by two turtle-doves or two pigeons, the first serving for the *ḥaṭṭā'ṯ* sacrifice and the second being offered as a holocaust; they may even content themselves with an offering of flour without oil or incense (Lev. v. 7–13).

In the rites this sacrifice is distinguished from the others by two traits: the function of the blood and the using of the flesh of the victim. It is the sacrifice in which blood plays the most important part. If the sacrifice is offered for the high-priest or for all the people, there are three rites in succession: having gathered the blood, the officiant enters the Holy Place, and seven times makes a sprinkling before the veil which shuts off the Holy of Holies, then he rubs with blood the horns of the altar of perfumes which is before the veil, and finally he pours the rest at the foot of the altar of holocausts. These are the only bloody sacrifices where something of the victim is introduced inside the Temple. For the sin of the 'prince' leader or for that of an individual, there is simply a rubbing of the horns of the altar of holocausts (outside the Temple) and the rest of the blood is poured at the foot of the altar; in these two sacrifices nothing of the victim enters the Holy Place.

(1924), pp. 51–69; id., art. 'Expiation', in *Supplément au dictionnaire de la Bible* iv (1938), cols. 48–81; D. Schötz, *Schuld- und Sündopfer im Alten Testament* (1930); R. Dussaud, *Les Origines cananéennes du sacrifice israélite*[2] (1941), pp. 117–29; L. Moraldi, *Espiazione sacrificale e riti espiatori nell'ambiente biblico e nell'Antico Testamento* (1956), pp. 109–81.

[2] 'Anointed priest' is a term for the high-priest at the post-exilic period, Lev. vi. 13 (EVV. 20) (keep the singular with the Hebrew), 15 (EVV. 22); xvi. 32, xxi. 10 (addition); cf. the ceremony of investiture, Exod. xxix. 7; Lev. viii. 12.

These rites manifestly stress the expiatory value of the blood. According to the Hebrew conception, the blood contains the life, it is life itself (Gen. ix. 4; Lev. vii. 26–27; Deut. xii. 23). 'The life of the flesh is in the blood. This blood I have given it to you, [I have done this] so that you may on the altar perform the rite of expiation for your lives; for it is the blood which expiates by the life which is in it' (Lev. xvii. 11). The last words are sometimes translated 'which expiates for a life', yet grammar and context favour the translation which we have adopted: there is no question in this passage of the substitution of the victim for the offerer, nor any question of the life of an offerer; the concern is with the life of the victim, which is its blood (verses 11*a* and 14). Blood expiates because it has or because it is life.[3] This text inspired the Epistle to the Hebrews, which applies it to the sacrifice of Christ: 'without shedding of blood there is no remission' (Heb. ix. 22). The equivalent of this is found later in the rabbinic saying: 'no expiation except in blood'.[4]

All the fat of the victim is burnt on the altar, as with the sacrifice of communion, but there is a different distribution of the fleshy parts. The offerer who recognizes his guilt has no share in it and all goes to the priests. However, when the *ḥaṭṭā'ṯ* sacrifice is offered for the sin of the community or for that of the high-priest who represents the community, the priests themselves can eat nothing of the victim; the latter is carried outside the sanctuary and burnt upon the heap of ashes (Lev. iv. 11–12, 21, vii. 17–23). Rather different dispositions are presupposed for the ritual of investiture of priests. A calf (and not an ox) is offered for the sin of Aaron (Lev. ix. 8–11), a he-goat (and not an ox) is offered for the sin of the people (Lev. ix. 15), and it is not said that the blood thereof is carried inside the

[3] With this meaning A. Metzinger concurs, in 'Die Substitutionstheorie und das alttestamentliche Opfer mit besonderer Berücksichtigung von Lev. 17. 11', in *Biblica* xxi (1940), pp. 159–87, 247–72, 335–7, especially pp. 257–72; L. Moraldi, *Espiazione* . . ., pp. 237–43; J. E. Steinmueller, 'Sacrificial Blood in the Bible', in *Biblica* xl (1959), pp. 556–67, especially p. 561; S. Lyonnet, 'De munere sacrificali sanguinis', in *Verbum Domini* xxxix (1961), pp. 18–38, especially pp. 26–32.

[4] Talmud Bab., Yoma 5*a*; Zebaḥim 6*a*; Menaḥot 93*b*.

sanctuary; the two victims are burnt. The short *midrash* of Leviticus x. 16–20 was drawn up later to make Leviticus ix. 15 tally with Leviticus vi. 22–23 (EVV. 29–30), yet the explanation is hardly lucid.

The fact that the fat elements are burnt upon the altar and that the flesh of sacrifices for sins of individuals is eaten by the priests 'as a very holy thing' (Lev. vi. 22) (EVV. 29) contradicts the theory which has it that the victim would be laden with the sin of the offerer and would undergo the penalty that was due to him.[5] No, the victim does not become 'sin'; it is pleasing to God, who in consideration for this offering removes the sin. It is patently in this ritual sense that the word is used by St. Paul: 'Christ did not know sin, God made him "sin" (*ḥaṭṭā'ṯ*)', i.e. 'victim for sin', 2 Corinthians v. 21.[6]

Prescriptions rather different from those of Leviticus are given by Numbers xv. 22–29. In this text the sin of the high-priest and that of the prince are not considered and it is a question only of the sin of the community or of an individual; inadvertent faults of the community are wiped out by the holocaust of an ox and the sacrifice *ḥaṭṭā'ṯ* of a he-goat, the inadvertent faults of an individual are wiped out by the sacrifice *ḥaṭṭā'ṯ* of a young goat. Details of the rites are not given. When it is a matter of deliberate fault,[7] it cannot be expiated by a sacrifice and the guilty one must be cut off from the community.[8]

[5] This theory of a penal vicarious substitution has been specially developed by A. Médebielle, *L'Expiation* . . ., pp. 114–75; id., art. 'Expiation', in *Supplément au dictionnaire de la Bible* iii (1938), cols. 74–81, yet elements of it are found in authors of very different tendencies: E. Dhorme, *La Religion des Hébreux nomades* (1937), pp. 215–19; W. O. E. Oesterley, *Sacrifices in Ancient Israel* (1937), pp. 225 f.; A. Clamer, *Le Lévitique* (1940), pp. 22 f.; H. Cazelles, *Le Lévitique*[2] (1958), pp. 12 f.; O. Procksch, *Theologie des Alten Testaments* (1950), pp. 558–61. Arguments contrary to this theory have been specially developed by A. Metzinger, 'Die Substitutionstheorie . . .'; L. Moraldi, *Espiazione* . . ., pp. 95–98; L. Sabourin, *Rédemption sacrificielle. Une enquête exégétique* (1961), pp. 174–84.

[6] The history of the exegesis of this text has been lengthily set out by L. Sabourin, *Rédemption sacrificielle* . . ., pp. 11–160.

[7] The sin committed 'high handedly', *b^eyāḏ rāmāh*, is more than a conscious fault: it proceeds 'from a heart revolted against God and against His law', cf. 1 Sam. iii. 14.

[8] So, too, in the Rule of the Community at Qumrân, 1. *QS*. viii. 20–ix. 3,

These dispositions are sometimes thought to be anterior to those of Leviticus.[9] This is possible as regards the content, but, from the literary point of view, the passage from Numbers appears to be the more recent.[10]

The priestly texts mention or prescribe the *ḥaṭṭā'ṯ* sacrifice in numerous circumstances: for the consecration of the altar and of the priests (Exod. xxix. 10–14, 36; Lev. viii. 14–17), the entry upon priestly functions (Lev. ix. 8–11, 15), the consecration of Levites (Num. viii. 12), the purification of the woman after childbirth (Lev. xii. 6, 8), of the leper (Lev. xiv. 19), of the man with a seminal issue (Lev. xv. 15), of the woman with an issue of blood (Lev. xv. 29–30), for the Nazirite who has contracted an impurity (Num. vi. 11), and at the term of his consecration (Num. vi. 14).

The liturgical calendar of Numbers xxviii–xxix allows for *ḥaṭṭā'ṯ* sacrifices for the new moon (xxviii. 15), for the Passover (xxviii. 22), for the feast of Weeks (xxviii. 30), for the feast of Acclamations (xxix. 5), and on each of the eight days of the feast of Booths (xxix. 16–38). But the feast on which this sacrifice fills the essential place is that of the Day of Atonement.

II. *The Day of Atonement*[11]

The ritual is contained in Leviticus xvi. The text has been several times worked over. There are doublets, verses 6 and 11, 9*b* and 15, 4 and 32; verses 2 and 3 do not follow, and on the contrary verse 4 unduly separates verses 3 and 5, &c. There are two conclusions, verses 29*a* and 34; verses 29*b*–34 are an

faults committed 'high-handedly' against the law involve cutting off from the community; faults from inadvertence are punished by temporary exclusion.

[9] R. Rendtorff, *Die Gesetze in der Priesterschrift* (1954), pp. 14–17.

[10] Cf. K. Koch, *Die Priesterschrift von Exodus 25 bis Leviticus 16* (1959), pp. 57–58, n. 4.

[11] Cf. especially S. Landersdorfer, *Studien zum biblischen Versöhnungstag* (Alttestamentliche Abhandlungen, x. 1) (1924); M. Löhr, *Das Ritual von Lev. 16* (Schriften der Königsberger Gelehrten Gesellschaft, II. 1) (1925). Add, for the literary criticism, G. von Rad, *Die Priesterschrift im Hexateuch* (1934), pp. 85–88; Rendtorff, op. cit., pp. 59–62; Koch, op. cit., pp. 92–96.

addition which recalls the law of Leviticus xxiii. 27–32 and comments on the preceding ritual.

This ritual combines two ceremonies which differ in spirit and in origin. There is first of all a levitical ritual. The high-priest offers an ox in sacrifice for his sin and that of his 'house', i.e. the priests of Aaron. He penetrates—the only time in the year—behind the veil which shuts off the Holy of Holies, he incenses the propitiatory *kappōreṯ*, and sprinkles it with the blood of the ox. He then sacrifices a he-goat for the sin of the people, and carries its blood behind the veil, where he sprinkles the propitiatory, as he had done with the blood of the ox (verse 15). This expiation for the sins of the priesthood and of the people is linked, in a manner which seems artificial, to an expiation for the sanctuary, especially the altar, which is rubbed and sprinkled with the blood of ox and he-goat (verses 16–19). The two expiations are likewise united in the final addition (verse 33), but the terms are inverted.

To this ritual, which conforms to the rules and ideas of Leviticus, is added a particular rite which stems from other conceptions. The community offers two he-goats. These are drawn by lot, one for Yahweh, one for *ʿᵃzāʾzēl*. The goat for Yahweh serves for the sacrifice for the sins of the people, of which we have just spoken. This ceremony being accomplished, the other goat, still alive, is placed 'before Yahweh'; the high-priest places both hands on the head of the goat and confesses over it all the faults, voluntary or not, of the Israelites.[12] A man then leads the goat to the desert, and the goat takes itself off with all the sins of the people (verses 8–10, 20–22).

In the matter of the transfer of the fault, or stain, or illness to an animal which is made to disappear, scholars have collected many rites which are more or less similar in primitive cultures and folklore.[13] There is no need to go outside the Bible for an analogy; in the ritual for leprosy, a living bird, loosed in the

[12] This imposition of two hands with a confession of sin differs from an imposition of the hand on the head of a victim in a holocaust or communion sacrifice. Cf. p. 28.

[13] Especially J. G. Frazer, *The Scapegoat*[3] (1933).

open country, carries off the ill and the leper is declared pure (Lev. xiv. 2–9).[14]

But there is, in the rite of the Day of Atonement, something more. The term 'scapegoat' is an interpretation of the Septuagint and the Vulgate. In the Hebrew the goat is destined 'to *'ᵃzā'zēl*'. Recently G. R. Driver has sought in this word a common noun, as did the Greek and Latin versions. The word would mean 'the precipice' and would be the name of the place where the goat was led.[15] The philological basis of this hypothesis is debatable.[16] And, anyway, it ill accords with the text: the high-priest draws by lot two goats; one is 'for Yahweh', the other 'for *'ᵃzā'zēl*'; the parallelism is insufficient if we translate the second term by 'for the Precipice', and it needs also to be a personal name. So it is much more probable that it is the name of a supernatural being, of the demon Azazel. Thus was it understood by the Syriac version and the Targum, and even the book of Enoch, which makes Azazel the prince of demons relegated to the desert.[17]

In admitting this ancient custom, whose origin is unknown, the levitical ritual has exorcized it. The efficacy of the transfer of faults and the expiation which results from it are attributed to Yahweh, before whom the goat is first of all presented (verse 10). It is not sacrificed to Azazel, nor is it sacrificed to Yahweh, because, being laden with the sins of the people, it has become impure and cannot serve as a sacrificial victim.

[14] The parallelism is the more striking as this ritual of leprosy combines, as does that of the Day of Atonement, levitical prescriptions (a *ḥaṭṭā'ṯ* sacrifice, an *'āšām* sacrifice, a holocaust) and old superstitious rites.

[15] G. R. Driver, 'Three Technical Terms in the Pentateuch', in *J.S.S.* i (1956), pp. 97–98.

[16] Driver starts from an indication in the Mishnah, Yoma, vi. 8 (cf. Targum Ps.-Jon. on Lev. xvi. 10), according to which the goat was led to *bêṯ ḥaddûḏû*, 'the rocky place', which would correspond to the Beit Ḫûdêdûn of the present day. Cf. C. Schick, *Z.D.P.V.* iii (1880), pp. 214–19. But the text is not certain. The geographical name has been transmitted in various forms, the best of which seems to be *bêṯ ḥᵃrûḏûn*, which corresponds to Ḫirbet Ḫareidân towering over the valley of the Kidron about 4½ miles from Jerusalem. Cf. C. Clermont-Ganneau, in *Revue archéologique* (1881), p. 61; *Encyclopaedia Judaica* iv, cols. 396–7; F. M. Abel, *Géographie de la Palestine II* (1958), p. 273.

[17] Enoch ix. 6, x. 4–8. On desert places as sojourn of demons cf. Isa. xiii. 21, xxiv. 11–14; cf. Tobit viii. 3; Matt. xii. 43.

III. *Sacrifice of Reparation*

The other type of expiatory sacrifice is the *'āšām*. The word means the offence, then the means of repairing this offence, and finally the sacrifice of reparation. The sacrificial code has less about this sacrifice (Lev. v. 14–16, vii. 1–6), and says that the rites are the same as those for the sacrifice for sin (Lev. vii. 7). Yet this sacrifice is only envisaged for individuals, and, consequently, the blood of the victim is never carried into the Holy Place nor is the victim burnt outside the sanctuary. Moreover, the only victim mentioned is the ram. Finally this sacrifice has a fine added to it in the cases foreseen by Leviticus v. 14–16, 21–26 (EVV. vi. 2–7); Numbers v. 5–8: if the rights of God or one's neighbour have been infringed by damage which can be estimated in money, the guilty party, over and above the ram offered as a sacrifice of reparation, is to restore to the priests who represent Yahweh, or to the damaged person, the amount of the damage plus one-fifth. We should stress, however, that this restitution takes place apart from the sacrificial action.

The sacrifice of reparation is no part of the ritual of any of the great feasts. Outside the cases foreseen by the sacrificial code and by Numbers v. 5–8, it is prescribed (together with a *ḥaṭṭā'ṯ* sacrifice) for the cleansing of a leper (Lev. xiv. 10–28), after a sexual fault committed with a slave concubine of another man (Lev. xix. 21–22), and for the reconsecration of a Nazirite who has contracted an impurity and has purified himself with a *ḥaṭṭā'ṯ* sacrifice (Num. vi. 12).

IV. *Distinction between Sacrifice for Sin and Reparation Sacrifice*

It is very difficult to determine what it is that distinguishes these two kinds of sacrifice. In antiquity the point of the distinction was already lost. Philo[18] thought that the *ḥaṭṭā'ṯ* was an expiation of involuntary faults against one's neighbour, the

[18] *De Special. Legibus*, i, *De Victimis*, ii.

'āšām an expiation of involuntary faults against God and of all voluntary faults. According to Josephus[19] the distinction was between sins committed without witnesses and sins committed before witnesses. Origen made the difference lie in the gravity of the sin: *ḥaṭṭā'ṯ* for faults which deserved death, *'āšām* for faults which did not deserve it.[20] St. Augustine defines *peccatum* as a sin committed, *delictum* as a sin of omission, or else the first as a voluntary fault and the second as an involuntary fault.[21] St. Gregory the Great accepts St. Augustine's first definition while adding that *delictum* can be simply a fault in intention.[22]

Modern opinions are usually better founded, but are just as varied. Let us cite a few recent authors only. According to Médebielle[23] the *'āšām* is specially intended for the reparation of wrongs done to rights of property, divine or human, and it adds to the fundamental idea of expiation, already expressed by *ḥaṭṭā'ṯ*, that of a more rigorous satisfaction. Schötz[24] deems that *'āšām* expiates a fault against the divinity that is a sacrilegious act. According to Cazelles[25] the *'āšām* is offered in cases of involuntary infringement of the rights of the divinity, the *ḥaṭṭā'ṯ* for faults against one's neighbour but in relation with the law of Yahweh which condemns them. Saydon,[26] under the heading of expiation, distinguishes three kinds of fault: (1) faults which are 'high-handed', with contempt of the law: they cannot be expiated (Num. xv. 30); (2) ordinary faults committed with more or less consent but which are the effects of human frailty without perversity of will: these are expiated by the sacrifice for sin; (3) faults of ignorance or inadvertence: these are expiated by the reparation sacrifice. Moraldi[27] concludes that the two sacrifices

19 *Ant.* III. ix. 3.

20 Migne, *P.G.* xii, col. 453.

21 *Quaest. in Hept.* i. 3, qu. 29, Migne, *P.L.* xxxiv, cols. 681–2.

22 Migne, *P.L.* lxxvi, col. 1043.

23 A. Médebielle, *L'Expiation . . .*, pp. 57, 61.

24 D. Schötz, *Schuld- und Sündopfer im Alten Testament*, pp. 32–35, 45.

25 H. Cazelles, *Le Lévitique*², p. 12.

26 P. P. Saydon, 'Sin Offering and Trespass-Offering', in *C.B.Q.* viii (1946), pp. 393–8.

27 L. Moraldi, *Espiazione sacrificale . . .*, p. 180; id., 'Espiazione nell' Antico e nel Nuovo Testamento', in *Rivista Biblica* ix (1961), p. 295.

are equally intended for the expiation of sin, but that in *ḥaṭṭā'ṯ* the dominant aspect is that of expiation, and that in *'āšām* the dominant aspect is that of reparation; in neither case are voluntary faults at issue. Other authors, perhaps more wisely, give up trying to establish a distinction.[28]

In fact, if we limit ourselves to the cases which are envisaged in Leviticus iv–v, we get an impression that the *ḥaṭṭā'ṯ* covers a wider field, and that the *'āšām* is specially concerned with the faults by which God (or His priests) or the neighbour have been frustrated, which gives to this sacrifice its reparation character. But, within the sacrificial code itself, there are inconsistencies: the *ḥaṭṭā'ṯ* is also called *'āšām* in Leviticus v. 6–7; the *ḥaṭṭā'ṯ* is offered if one sins inadvertently against one or other of the commandments of Yahweh (Lev. iv. 2), but then the *'āšām* is also offered if one has done, without perceiving it, one of the things forbidden by the law of Yahweh (Lev. v. 17). Thus the two sacrifices have the same very general bearing. Further, the two are foreseen for cases very similar in type: the *ḥaṭṭā'ṯ* for him who evades the testimony which he ought to give before a judge, or who makes, under oath, a thoughtless declaration (Lev. v. 1, 4),[29] the *'āšām* for him who takes a false oath (Lev. v. 22, 24) (EVV. vi. 3, 5).

Confusion grows when we juxtapose the sacrificial code and certain special laws. The purification of the leper calls for an *'āšām* sacrifice, a *ḥaṭṭā'ṯ* sacrifice, and a holocaust (Lev. xiv. 10–32). So, too, the Nazirite who has made himself unclean by contact with a corpse must offer two turtle-doves or pigeons, one for a *ḥaṭṭā'ṯ* sacrifice, the other for a holocaust, and then a lamb in *'āšām* sacrifice (Num. vi. 9–12). The same uncertainty covers the moral aspect of the act which is to be expiated by these sacrifices: *ḥaṭṭā'ṯ* and *'āšām* are offered for sins of inadvertence. This is repeated in Leviticus iv. 13, 22, 27; v. 15, 17 (cf. Num. xv. 22–29). Yet examples are given of the two sacrifices in cases

[28] G. B. Gray, *Sacrifice . . .*, pp. 57–61; J. Pedersen, *Israel: Its Life and Culture III–IV*^{2} (1959), pp. 369–74.

[29] On the difficult passage of Lev. v. 1–6 cf. A. Spiro, in *Proceedings of the American Academy for Jewish Research* xxviii (1959), pp. 95–101.

which cannot be simple inadvertence, as with the *ḥaṭṭā'ṯ* for refusal to witness before a judge (Lev. v. 1), and *'āšām* for fraudulence in the matter of a deposit or of an object found (Lev. v. 21–22) (EVV. vi. 2–3).

These confusions and uncertainties are not sufficiently resolved by literary criticism.[30] Leviticus iv–v, generally, is composed, seemingly, of texts of different periods. The ritual of sacrifice for sin developed around a core constituted by Leviticus iv. 22–35, which concerns the sins of the chief or the individual. When this ritual was inserted into the sacrificial code, the sacrifice for the sin of the community was added (Lev. iv. 13–21). The special cases of Leviticus v. 1–6, and the prescriptions of Leviticus v. 7–13, which round off what concerns the sacrifice offered by an individual, are later additions, and it is in these passages that *ḥaṭṭā'ṯ* and *'āšām* are mentioned together (Lev. v. 6 and 7). The most recent passage would be that concerning the sin of the high-priest (Lev. iv. 3–12). In the ritual for the reparation sacrifice, the text of Leviticus v. 20–26 (EVV. vi. 1–7), with its new introduction, must be distinguished from Leviticus v. 14–16; verses 17–19, of a very general character, seem to have yet another origin. The whole section on the reparation sacrifice is differently constructed from that on sacrifice for sin. This latter orders the sacrifices according to the quality of those for whom they are offered, the former enumerates the cases when a sacrifice must be made. Between the two, Leviticus v. 1–6 is transitional: the passage is constructed like the section on the reparation sacrifice, but is concerned with particular cases of sacrifices for sin, which, moreover, is called a sacrifice of reparation in verse 6.

This analysis is hypothetical, but it is clear that in the final redaction the sacrifice for sin was set out in a more systematic and developed way than the sacrifice of reparation. This does not allow us to determine the relative age of each sacrificial form,

[30] Cf. in particular R. Rendtorff, *Die Gesetze in der Priesterschrift*, especially pp. 4–38; K. Koch, *Die Priesterschrift von Exodus 25 bis Leviticus 16*, especially pp. 45–67; K. Elliger, 'Zur Analyse des Sündopfergesetzes', in *Verbannung und Heimkehr* (*Festschrift Rudolph*) (1961), pp. 39–50.

but it does mean that at the period of the redaction of these texts, the sacrifice for sin had a greater importance; this is confirmed by the liturgy of the great feasts, which only retained the sacrifice for sin.

Whatever we make of the literary analysis, the juxtaposition in Leviticus of prescriptions which are often parallel concerning the *ḥaṭṭā'ṯ* and the *'āšām*, and the resultant confusion, show that the last redactors no longer knew exactly what specified the *ḥaṭṭā'ṯ* and the *'āšām*; or else they wanted to distinguish terms which were originally synonymous, or they confused the terms whose exact force they no longer knew.

v. *Historical Development*

Everyone recognizes that these legislative texts on expiatory sacrifices are late redactions. Since Wellhausen, many critics go further and are of the opinion that the very institution of these sacrifices is late. These sacrifices would not have been known before the Exile.

The *ḥaṭṭā'ṯ* sacrifice is mentioned several times in the historical books written after the Exile. Twelve he-goats were offered in sacrifice for sin at the dedication of the Second Temple (Ezra vi. 17), and also by the exiled people coming back with Ezra (Ezra viii. 35). Under Nehemiah, the community undertakes to pay the dues for the Temple service, which includes sacrifices for sin (Neh. x. 34). Finally, when describing Hezekiah's religious reform, 2 Chronicles xxix. 21–24 speaks of seven he-goats offered in sacrifice for sin 'for the monarchy, for the sanctuary, and for Judah'; after the imposition of hands, they are sacrificed and their blood is poured upon the altar. The Chronicler here draws his inspiration from the usages of the Second Temple. The *'āšām* sacrifice is mentioned only once (Ezra x. 19): Jews guilty of having wedded foreign wives must offer a ram in reparation sacrifice.[31]

[31] The Hebrew text has 'and they were guilty', but the phrase is badly constructed, and the correction 'and their *'āšām*' is called for by the Greek and by the parallel in 3 Esdras ix. 20 (EVV. 1 Esdras ix. 20).

The two kinds of sacrifice take up an important place in the plan of religious restoration which is traced in the last chapters of Ezekiel. The *ḥaṭṭā'ṯ* and *'āšām* are mentioned together in Ezekiel xl. 39, xlii. 13, xliv. 29, xlvi. 20. Further, *ḥaṭṭā'ṯ* sacrifices are prescribed during seven days for the consecration of the altar (Ezek. xliii. 18–26). A priest who has made himself unclean by contact with a dead person in his family must offer a sacrifice for sin (Ezek. xliv. 27). Several sacrifices for sin are ordered on the occasion of the Passover: the first day of the month, an ox for the sin of the sanctuary, with a special ritual (the corners of the altar base, the posts of the Temple, and those of the porch of the inner court are rubbed with the blood of the victim); this sacrifice is repeated on the seventh day of the month for whoever has sinned by inadvertence; on Passover day, an ox as sacrifice for sin; the seven days of the feast of Unleavened Bread, a goat as sacrifice for sin (Ezek. xlv. 18–24). On the other hand, apart from the texts where the two forms of sacrifice are mentioned together and which have been cited above, no details are ever given about the *'āšām* sacrifice, nor on the circumstances in which it should be offered.

From these texts, the conclusion has been reached that expiatory sacrifices were an institution of the exilic period. It would be strange, however—to say no more—that new forms of cult should have been invented during the Exile, during which no external cult was practised. We should note also that Ezekiel does not explain what the *ḥaṭṭā'ṯ* is, nor the *'āšām*; he seems to suppose that the terms are known. He does not give the detail of their ritual (except for the sacrifice of the first day of the first month (Ezek. xlv. 19)), which seems to point to this ritual being known. These conclusions are particularly true of the *'āšām*, which is mentioned several times without any detail: this is not the way in which an innovation is introduced. Moreover, we have noted the uncertainties of the ritual in relation to these sacrifices and their distinction. These uncertainties are better explained if the ritual is taking up again some ancient elements whose precise significance are no longer known.

An objection is that the last legislative text before the Exile, Deuteronomy, mentions the holocaust and the sacrifice of communion, but says nothing of expiatory sacrifices—and the conclusion is drawn that these expiatory sacrifices were instituted later. But Deuteronomy contains no sacrificial law at all, and mentions the holocaust and communion sacrifice only occasionally; it has no more to say either about cereal offerings or incense, or the shew-bread, which were surely all part of pre-exilic worship. Moreover, it is not true that Deuteronomy is the only legislative text which represents the religious situation just before the Exile. There is another body of legislation which, better than Deuteronomy, represents the usages of the Temple at Jerusalem at the end of the monarchy—I mean the Holiness Code.[32] No more than Deuteronomy does the Holiness Code include a sacrificial code, but it is there that we find the most explicit text on the expiatory value of the sacrifices (Lev. xvii. 11), and the *'āšām* sacrifice is here prescribed for a particular case (Lev. xix. 20–22).

Some older indications could be adduced, but they are contested. Recording Jehoash's ordinances concerning the Temple, 2 Kings xii. 17 (EVV. 16) says that 'the money of the *'āšām* and of the *ḥaṭṭā'ṯ*[33] was not handed over to the Temple of Yahweh, it was for the priests'. It is hard to decide if it is a matter of fines for faults analogous to those which were deleted by *ḥaṭṭā'ṯ* and *'āšām* sacrifices, or of taxes which went with the sacrifices, or of payments which dispensed with them. But it is significant that this money goes to the priests, as does the flesh of victims offered in sacrifices of the same name, according to the ritual of Leviticus. In this text, *'āšām* and *ḥaṭṭā'ṯ* are certainly terms of cult language. Now, in the development of

[32] R. de Vaux, *Ancient Israel: Its Life and Institutions*, pp. 144, 472. W. Kornfeld, *Studien zum Heiligkeitsgesetz* (1952), pp. 11–12; H. Cazelles, *Le Lévitique*, pp. 16–17. For the ancient character of the Law of Holiness see most recently H. Reventlow, *Das Heiligkeitsgesetz, formgeschichtlich untersucht* (1961), pp. 165–6, at the end of a study whose method is, on another score, open to criticism.

[33] The singular must be read with the Greek, as opposed to the plural of the Hebrew.

worship, it is not a monetary fine which is replaced by a sacrificed victim, it is the reverse process which is normal.[34] These sacrifices would thus be old. If mention is made of taxes which were added to these sacrifices, as in the legislation of Leviticus v. 14–26 (EVV. v. 14–19, vi. 1–7); Numbers v. 5–8, these then evidently presuppose the existence of the sacrifices themselves.

The text of Hosea iv. 8 is much less conclusive: 'they sate themselves on the sin, *ḥaṭṭā'ṯ*,[35] of my people and are avid of its iniquity, *'āwôn*'. Seeing that *ḥaṭṭā'ṯ* means all at once the sacrifice for sin and the victim of that sacrifice, and that the flesh of this victim has been eaten by the priests (Lev. vi. 19) (EVV. 26), one can find here a reference to sacrifice for sin.[36] Nevertheless, the parallelism with 'iniquity', *'āwôn*, which is not a ritual term,[37] favours another exegesis:[38] the priests and the people practise a cult which is not approved by God, cf. the immediate context Hosea iv. 4–7, 12–13, and the other texts of the prophet (Hos. viii. 11, 13): a 'sin', an 'iniquity'. However, it remains possible that *'āwôn* is only introduced here for the parallelism and that *ḥaṭṭā'ṯ* is employed with the double sense of 'sin' and 'sacrifice for sin'.[39]

A final text is sometimes used to prove the antiquity of the sacrifice for sin; it is that of Micah: 'shall I have to offer my eldest son foı .my misdeed, *peša'*, the fruit of my bowels for my sin, *ḥaṭṭā'ṯ*?' (Mic. vi. 7).[40] It might suggest a sacrifice for sin,

[34] In the same sense, cf. D. Schötz, *Schuld- und Sündopfer . . .*, p. 119; W. Eichrodt, *Theologie des Alten Testaments*[6], p. 57, n. 321.

[35] The Greek and Latin have the plural.

[36] This has been admitted by a certain number of commentators, and by E. Sellin, *Beiträge zur israelitischen und jüdischen Religionsgeschichte* i (1896), pp. 160–1, n. 2; ii (1897), pp. 303–4, n. 2; E. König, *Theologie des Alten Testaments*[3–4] (1923), p. 290; O. Procksch, *Theologie des Alten Testaments* (1949), pp. 553, 557, 656; R. Vuilleumier, *La Tradition cultuelle d'Israël dans la prophétie d'Amos et d'Osée* (1960), p. 70.

[37] Unless we admit with Procksch, loc. cit., and even Sellin, loc. cit., that *'āwôn* is another name for the reparation sacrifice.

[38] Thus, particularly, W. R. Harper, *Amos and Hosea* (1910), and recently A. Weiser, *Das Buch der zwölf Kleinen Propheten I* (1949); H. W. Wolff, *Dodekapropheton I, Hosea* (1961).

[39] Cf. C. F. Keil, *Biblischer Commentar ueber die zwölf Kleinen Propheten* (1888).

[40] This is the meaning defended in particular by E. König, *Geschichte der*

but the parallelism with *peša'* makes this sense even less plausible than in Hosea iv. 8, because here *peša'* precedes *ḥaṭṭā'ṯ*.

Indications of the existence of the sacrifice for sin and the reparation sacrifice before the Exile are thus rare and debatable, the most conclusive being 2 Kings xii. 17 (EVV. 16), and the Law of Holiness, if we accept the date I have suggested for the latter. Yet we need to remember that references to these sacrifices are also very rare in the historical books later than the Exile, at a period when they certainly existed. The silence of pre-exilic texts does not lessen the force of the general argument which was first expounded: these sacrificial forms are assumed to be known by Ezekiel, so they could not have been invented during the Exile, hence they must go back further. We must, however, recognize that if these expiatory sacrifices existed, they were less frequent than the holocaust and especially less frequent than the sacrifice of communion. They are derivative forms, which assumed a greater importance when the great national calamities had given to the people a livelier sense of their culpability and when a finer sense of Yahweh's claims and of the gravity of sin had developed.

VI. *Expiatory Sacrifices among Israel's Neighbours*

1. *Mesopotamia*

For the Babylonians and Assyrians, all evil, physical or otherwise, individual or not, is the punishment of a fault, voluntary or involuntary, which has angered the divinity. The divinity turns away from the guilty party and abandons him to malefic powers, demons or sorcerers, who seize upon him and make him suffer. To obtain deliverance from evil, one must 'calm the heart' of the gods and reduce evil forces to powerlessness. This is the aim of exorcisms, which occupy so large a place in cuneiform

alttestamentlichen Religion (1912), p. 234; A. Médebielle, *L'Expiation . . .*, p. 63; deemed 'plausible' by O. Procksch, op. cit., pp. 553, 557, 656. This last author consequently interprets *peša'* as another designation of the reparation sacrifice.

literature.[41] These exorcisms were practised by a special category of priests, the *âshipu*, 'conjurator', assisted eventually by the *kalû*, 'lamentator', and the *mashmashu*, 'purifier'. The essential parts of the ceremony were the confession of sins, conscious or unconscious, for which long lists were drawn up; prayer, asking for the help of the gods, and in particular the 'penitential psalms'; and finally the conjuration which was calculated to expel the demon and make the evil disappear. This conjuration included formulae and rites.[42] The texts and ritual actions consist of a mixture of real religious feeling and of magical practices. But the idea of expiation is not expressed: it does not exist in the religions of Mesopotamia.[43]

Certain scholars, however, consider expiatory the sacrifices termed 'substitution' sacrifices:[44] the *âshipu* priest would immolate, with appropriate formulae, an animal which would be considered the substitute of the sick person. The danger was then averted and the sick person healed. But these are not sacrifices: the animal was handed over to the devil for him to do his worst with it and leave the man; no expiatory value whatever is attached to this operation, which belongs much more to magic than to religion.[45] Mesopotamia did not know an equivalent of the sacrifice for sin.[46]

There is, however, a Babylonian rite which recalls one aspect of the Israelite Day of Expiations. On the fifth day of the New Year feast at Babylon, the incantator would purify the sanctuaries of Bêl and Nabû with water, oil, and scents, then a sacrificer would cut off the head of a sheep and rub with its carcass the Temple of Nabû so as to efface its impurities. The incantator

[41] Especially in the two great treatises *Shurpu* and *Maqlu*.

[42] W. Schrank, *Babylonische Sühnriten besonders mit Rücksicht auf Priester und Büsser* (1908); E. Dhorme, *Les Religions de Babylonie et d'Assyrie* (1945), pp. 258–71; J. Bottéro, *La Religion babylonienne* (1952), pp. 129–32.

[43] Cf. W. Schrank, op. cit., p. 88; Ch. F. Jean, *Le Péché chez les Babyloniens et les Assyriens* (1925), p. 11.

[44] B. Meissner, *Babylonien und Assyrien* ii (1925), pp. 83 f.; E. Dhorme, op. cit., pp. 229 f.; and cf. above, p. 56.

[45] G. Furlani, *Il sacrificio nella religione dei Semiti di Babilonia e Assiria* (1932), pp. 180 f.; L. Moraldi, *Espiazione . . .*, p. 29, with other references.

[46] J. Bottéro, op. cit., p. 119.

and sacrificer would then go and throw into the Euphrates the head and carcass of the sheep and then withdraw into the country. They could only come back into town at the end of the feast, the 12th Nisan.[47] The Day of Expiations also included a purification of the sanctuary (Lev. xvi. 20), and the Babylonian rite outwardly resembles the ceremony of the emissary goat. The animal is led off, laden with impurities, and the ministers become impure on contact with it (Lev. xvi. 26). Yet the two rites are profoundly different: the 'scape-sheep' is slaughtered (not sacrificed) and it clears the sanctuary of its impurities, whereas the scapegoat plays no part in the purification of the sanctuary, and it is not killed. It carries away the sins of the people, an essential trait which is lacking in the Babylonian ritual.[48]

2. *The Hittites*

The situation is very similar with the Hittites, among whom magic plays an even more important part than in Mesopotamia. In Asia Minor analogous rites are found of substitution, of purification, and of exorcism; and sins are confessed.[49] There are, however, in the Hittite religion offerings and sacrifices which can be called 'expiatory' in the sense that, unlike the analogous rites of Mesopotamia, they are imposed as a punishment for the fault committed and as a reparation of the damage caused to the gods.[50] The Hittites also used to practise rites of transference recalling that of the scapegoat. An evil, as, for example, pest or plague, is ravaging the country or the army. This is transferred

[47] The text has been published by F. Thureau-Dangin, *Rituels Accadiens* (1921), pp. 140–1.

[48] Cf. S. Landersdorfer, 'Keilschriftliche Parallelen zum biblischen Sündenbock', in *B.Z.* xix (1931), pp. 20–28.

[49] Cf. R. Pettazoni, 'Confession of Sins in Hittite Religion', in *Orient and Occident* (*Gaster Anniversary Volume*) (1936), pp. 467–71.

[50] A. Götze, *Kleinasien*² (1957), p. 151; G. Furlani, *La Religione degli Hittiti* (1936), pp. 306, 365. The most important texts on the confession of sins and reparation for them are the two prayers of Muršiliš, edited and commented by A. Götze, 'Die Pestgebete des Muršiliš', in *Kleinasiatische Forschungen* i (1930), pp. 161–251; on the terms relating to expiation cf. especially pp. 190–2.

magically to an animal who is hounded out, generally beyond the frontiers, to the enemy whence the evil is deemed to have come.[51]

3. *The Arabs*

More useful information has been gathered in pre-islamic Arabia. At the present day we know ten or so inscriptions, nearly all Sabaean, whose object is the confession of sins.[52] At the end the penitent man (or rather woman, for all the inscriptions but two are drawn up for women) declares that he has humbled himself before the divinity and he has 'made a penitential offering'. These last words translate the verb *ḥâṭâ* used in the intensive form, as the corresponding form of the same verb in Hebrew in the sense of 'making an offering or a sacrifice for sin' (Lev. vi. 19 (EVV. 26), ix. 15). This penitential offering is accompanied by a fine, which is a new point of contact with Leviticus.

In the Minean colony of northern Arabia, at el-'Ela and at Medaïn Saleh, several inscriptions contain the term *ryt*, which is interpreted as 'expiatory offering'; it consists of goods or persons (once it is a hierodule) who are presented to the divinity. This word *ryt* is also found in the Mesha stele, and would seem to be patient of the same explanation; the translation would run: 'I have massacred all the population of the town as an expiatory offering to Kemosh and to Moab.'[53]

[51] A. Götze, *Kleinasien*, p. 159, with the references in n. 9: a few texts are summarized in G. Furlani, *La Religione degli Hittiti*, pp. 201–3; cf. also Landersdorfer, *B.Z.* xix (1931), pp. 20–28. An interesting text is cited by O. R. Gurney, *The Hittites* (1952), p. 162: 'They bring in a donkey and drive it towards the enemy's country and speak as follows: "Thou, O Yarris, hast inflicted evil on this country and its camp; but let this donkey lift it and carry it into the enemy's country." '

[52] R. Pettazoni, *La confessione dei peccati II*, 2 (1935), pp. 312–17; G. Ryckmans, 'Deux inscriptions expiatoires sabéennes', in *R.B.* xli (1932), pp. 393–7 (these are the inscriptions reproduced again in *Répertoire d'épigraphie sémitique* vii, nos. 3956 and 3957); id., 'La Confession publique des péchés en Arabie Méridionale préislamique', in *Le Muséon* lviii (1945), pp. 1–14. Cf. G. Ryckmans, *Les Religions arabes préislamiques*[3] (1960), p. 220.

[53] G. Ryckmans, *Les Religions arabes préislamiques*, p. 216; id., 'Het oude Arabia en de Bijbel', in *Jaarbericht Ex Oriente Lux* xiv (1955–6), p. 81. These are the texts found in *Répertoire d'épigraphie sémitique* vi, nos. 3282, 3345, 3346, 3356, 3603, 3697.

The interest of these parallels is diminished by the fact that the South Arabian inscriptions are all later than the sacerdotal texts of the Bible and that they treat of expiatory offerings and not of sacrifices. Expiatory sacrifice as such is not attested in pre-islamic Arabia.

4. *Canaan*

The Bible and inscriptions coming from Phoenicia proper do not say that the Canaanites knew of expiatory sacrifices. Yet some have thought to find them in the texts from Carthage and Ras Shamra.

The so-called Marseilles sacrificial tariff[54] calls *kll* a sacrifice in which a part of the victim came to the priest and nothing was given to the offerer. The conclusion drawn was that it was equivalent to the expiatory sacrifices of Leviticus in which the offerer received nothing, all the meat (other than the fat burnt on the altar) being eaten by the priests.[55] As we lack other details and are completely ignorant about the intention of this sacrifice, the equivalence is purely conjectural;[56] and at least the name is different from that of the Hebrew.[57] This doubt is augmented by the tariff of Carthage, in which, instead of *kll*, we have the plural *kllm*, which would appear to cover both expiatory sacrifice and holocaust, with, moreover, prescriptions which do not exactly fit one or the other according to the norms of Leviticus. We must recognize that the tariffs of Marseilles and of Carthage presuppose different sacrificial systems, and this diversity weakens still more the case for comparison with the Israelite sacrifice which has been attempted.

[54] Cf. above, p. 45.

[55] M.-J. Lagrange, *Études sur les religions sémitiques*² (1905), p. 472; R. Dussaud, *Les Origines cananéennes du sacrifice israélite*² (1941), pp. 142 f.; J. G. Février, 'Le Vocabulaire sacrificiel punique', in *J.A.* ccxliii (1955), p. 50; id., 'Remarques sur le grand tarif dit de Marseille', in *Cahiers de Byrsa* viii (1958–9), p. 37.

[56] D. M. L. Urie, 'Sacrifice among the West Semites', in *P.E.Q.* (1949), pp. 67–68.

[57] Unless we recognize an expiatory sacrifice in the *kālîl* of Deut. xxxiii. 10; Ps. li. 21 (EVV. 19), thus Dussaud, op. cit., p. 144, which is contradicted by 1 Sam. vii. 9, where *kālîl* stands for holocaust.

The term *kll* has also been read in a poem from Ras Shamra and interpreted by some as an 'expiatory sacrifice', in the light of the Marseilles tariff.[58] But this exegesis has not won acceptance: we should read *k-lli*, 'like a lamb'.[59] In several small texts from Ras Shamra, the word *a̱tm* has been explained by the Hebrew *'āšām* and translated 'sacrifice of reparation'.[60] But this word is only found in two very mutilated texts[61] which are untranslatable and are written in Hurrite rather than in a Semitic language.[62]

More important are ritual texts which relate remission of sin with sacrifice and with blood,[63] and which mention a payment of money as an offering of 'body and soul'.[64] The most significant is a text where, several times over, it is a matter of sin or transgression and thereupon of sacrifice of libation to the gods.[65] Unfortunately, this text is not patient of a continuous translation and it does not appear that sacrifice has as its end the expiation of a fault.

The results of this inquiry are not very conclusive, and are not sufficient to prove that, among the peoples who were neighbours of Israel, there existed expiatory sacrifices comparable to

[58] Gordon, **49.** II. 23, according to the interpretation of J. W. Jack, *The Ras Shamra Tablets. Their Bearing on the Old Testament* (1935), p. 30; R. Dussaud, *Les Origines . . .*, p. 327.

[59] W. Baumgartner, in *Theologische Rundschau*, N.F. xiii (1941), p. 97; cf. W. F. Albright, *Archaeology and the Religion of Israel*² (1946), p. 61.

[60] J. W. Jack, loc. cit.; Th. H. Gaster, 'The Service of the Sanctuary, A Study in Hebrew Survivals', in *Mélanges Syriens offerts à R. Dussaud II* (1939), p. 578. The hypothesis is accepted by W. Baumgartner, loc. cit., p. 97, and by Urie, loc. cit., p. 72.

[61] Gordon, **27**: *a̱tm* is found ten times at the beginning of lines in which only one word survives; **45.** 7: *a̱tm* is at the end of a line of which only two words survive, in a short text which only retains a word or part of a word in the other lines; perhaps also **34.** 8: *a̱t*.

[62] C. H. Gordon first of all explained *a̱tm* by the Hebrew *'āšām*, *Ugaritic Handbook* (1947), p. 46. Then he gave this up and considered the word to be Hurrite, ibid., p. 216, Glossary, no. 351. All references to this word have disappeared from the re-edition, *Ugaritic Manual* (1955). Cf. J. Gray, 'Cultic Affinities between Israel and Ras Shamra', in *Z.A.W.* lxii (1950), pp. 210–11; id., *The Legacy of Canaan* (Supplement to *V.T.* v) (1957), pp. 144–5.

[63] Gordon, **9.** 1.

[64] Gordon, **5.** 12, 15.

[65] Gordon, **2.** 14 f., 23 f., 31 f. Cf. A. De Guglielmo, 'Sacrifice in the Ugaritic Texts', in *C.B.Q.* xvii (1955), pp. 212–13.

those of the levitical ritual. This originality of Yahwist religion is a consequence of its moralism. Certainly the Israelites shared Eastern notions about the link between sin and physical evil, and they accepted superstitious customs which were deemed capable of wiping out uncleanness (ritual for leprosy, the scape-goat, &c.). But they had the notion of a fault as a transgression of the divine law; it was an offence against God and called for reparation. Pardon from God was obtained by contrition of heart. Such was the teaching of the prophets. But it was normal that this interior conviction should express itself and become efficacious by rites, and this is where expiatory sacrifices came in. We have tried to show that they are not a late institution, and that they existed before the Exile, and that their importance grew progressively. This evolution has its counterpart in a prophetic movement. Already during the Exile, Deutero-Isaiah describes the servant of Yahweh who is smitten because of the sins of the people, who is as a lamb for the slaughter (Isa. liii. 7), 'truly has he made himself an offering for reparation', *'āšām* (Isa. liii. 10).[66] Thus is a door opened upon the New Testament. Jesus is the 'Lamb of God who takes away the sins of the world' (John i. 29), 'Christ knew not sin, God has made him a victim for sin, *ḥaṭṭā'ṯ*, so that in him we might become justice of God' (2 Cor. v. 21).

[66] The text is difficult. I adopt the reading recently proposed by M. Dahood, *C.B.Q.* xxii (1960), p. 406. The ritual interpretation of *'āšām* in Isa. liii. 10 is now common, cf. E. Kissane, *The Book of Isaiah II* (1943), p. 190; C. R. North, *The Suffering Servant in Deutero-Isaiah*[2] (1956), p. 126; J. Scharbert, 'Stellvertretendes Sühneleiden in den Ebed-Jahwe-Liedern und in altorientalischen Ritualtexten', in *B.Z.* N.F. ii (1958), p. 210.

INDEX

(*a*) MODERN AUTHORS

Rost, L., 14, 39, 48, 64.
Rothstein, G., 54.
Rudolph, W., 2.
Ryckmans, G., 15, 16, 43, 109.

Sabourin, L., 94.
Savignac, R., 53.
Saydon, P. P., 99.
Scharbert, J., 38, 112.
Schick, C., 97.
Schneider, N., 55.
Schötz, D., 92, 99, 105.
Schrank, W., 107.
Segal, J. B., 26.
Sellin, E., 105.
Smith, S., 55.
Smith, W. Robertson, 17, 38, 43, 53.
Snaith, N. H., 30, 31, 42.
von Soden, W., 56, 58.
Spiro, A., 100.
Stade, B., 70.
Starcky, J., 57.
Steinmann, J., 68.
Steinmueller, J. E., 93.
Steve, M. J., 10.
Stevenson, W. B., 31.
Strobel, P., 24.
Sukenik, E. L., 13.

Talmon, S., 2.
Thureau-Dangin, F., 108.

Ungnad, A., 59.
Urie, D. M. L., 45, 46, 110, 111.

Van der Leeuw, G., 63.
de Vaux, R., 1, 2, 10, 12, 13, 19, 20, 22, 35, 60, 62, 64, 69, 76, 77, 104.
Vincent, A., 3, 32.
Vincent, L. H., 60.
Virolleaud, C., 86.
Volz, P., 28, 69, 73.
Vuilleumier, R., 105.

Waszink, J. H., 49.
Weidner, E., 47, 57, 86.
Weiser, A., 68, 73, 75, 105.
Wellhausen, J., 17, 43, 54, 71, 102.
Wendel, A., 39, 41.
Westermarck, E., 52.
Wolff, H. W., 68, 105.
Woolley, L., 55.

Yerkes, R. K., 48.

Zimmerli, W., 72, 87, 89.
Zimmern, H., 18, 72.
Zolli, I., 24.

INDEX

(*b*) SCRIPTURE REFERENCES